FRANCIS & CLARE
OF ASSISI

HarperCollins Spiritual Classics:

John of the Cross
Teresa of Avila
The Cloud of Unknowing
John and Charles Wesley
Meister Eckhart
Bonaventure: The Life of St. Francis
William Law
Quaker Spirituality
Bernard of Clairvaux
Hildegard of Bingen
Augustine of Hippo
Francis & Clare of Assisi

FRANCIS & CLARE OF ASSISI

Selected Writings

Foreword by Michael Morris

Translation by Regis J. Armstrong

and Ignatius C. Brady

Edited by Emilie Griffin

HarperSanFrancisco

A Division of HarperCollins*Publishers*

HarperCollins Web site: http://www.harpercollins.com
HarperCollins®, ♨®, and HarperSanFrancisco™ are trademarks of HarperCollins Publishers.

Book Design by Susan Rimerman

FIRST EDITION

Library of Congress Cataloging-in-Publication Data
Francis of Assisi, Saint, 1182–1226
  [Selections. English, 2006]
  Francis & Clare of Assisi: selected writings: foreword by Michael Morris; translated by Regis J. Armstrong and Ignatius C. Brady; edited by Emilie Griffin — 1st ed.
    p. cm.
  ISBN-13: 978–0–06–075465–5
  ISBN-10: 0–06–075465–6
    1. Catholic Church. 2. Theology. 3. Spiritual life—Catholic Church. I. Title: Francis and Clare of Assisi. II. Title: Selected Writings. III. Armstrong, Regis J. IV. Brady, Ignatius C.V. Griffin, Emilie. VI. Clare, of Assisi, Saint, 1194–1253. Selections. English. 2006. VII. Title.

BRX890.F665213 2006
230—dc22

06 07 08 09 10 RRD(H) 10 9 8 7 6 5 4 3 2 1

CONTENTS

FOREWORD

"Religious" is a label that I have never worn well. Many associates and friends have tried to describe me as such, but regardless of how well intended the description, the word always manages to irritate me. As I approach four decades on this earth, the one thing that I finally know about myself is that I am not religious. When I first became serious about having a relationship with Jesus Christ, I'd argue against the label, stating that I was a "spiritual Christian" as opposed to one who follows the regulations of religion.

The word "religious" brings to mind the Pharisees who followed doctrine but whose hearts were hardened against the truth. On the other hand, "spiritual" in the context of Christianity makes me think of the great saints of the faith who lived out the teachings of Jesus on a daily, hourly, and minute-by-minute basis. It makes me think of those like Saint Francis and Saint Clare of Assisi who not only wore their faith on their sleeves in the simplicity of their clothing, but who also wore it on their hearts through the deeds of their lives.

Growing up as a Southern Baptist, I encountered many "saints" in the church who lived out their faith in an active, tangible way. Often these individuals were older ladies to whom even the pastor would turn to when in need of prayer. Ministering behind the scenes, these ladies still can be found delivering the spiritually hungry to church, teaching Sunday School, and visiting those with physical and emotional infirmities. While reading the writings of

Saint Clare of Assisi, I thought of the women I'd known in that concrete-block Baptist church back in rural Florida. Like Saint Clare, those ladies could be described as complex individuals who learned how to mold themselves as steel fists inside delicate velvet gloves while at the same time molding and advancing church doctrine.

Saint Francis was instrumental in the direction of Saint Clare's life. When she was fleeing the threat of an arranged marriage, Saint Francis is credited with helping to direct her to the monastery of the Poor Ladies. There in a world of prayer and poverty, Saint Clare found a purpose higher than what the world could offer.

As a warrior of prayer, Saint Clare's miraculous faith was credited by the townspeople with twice saving their city from enemy attack. Long before she was formally canonized, Saint Clare had already become a saint in the hearts of the people of Assisi. A well-loved Christian leader whose writings remain a translucent image of her love of God and people, Saint Clare was a visionary who was not afraid of vocalizing what she believed, even if it meant disagreeing with church leadership. There is no greater example of this than the Rule of Clare, in which she courageously and successfully reinstated the utter vow of poverty that Pope Gregory IX had loosely defined for the monasteries of the Poor Ladies. Saint Clare opposed any doctrine that she viewed as weakening the intentions of Saint Francis to resist possessing any worldly goods.

The writings found within this volume speak to a longing deep within my spirit to run away from the worldly trappings of life in favor of a remote location void of cell phone coverage,

BlackBerry and e-mail connections, and reality television. I picture myself in a stone cottage tucked away in the corner of a forest lined with ferns and redwoods, praying and studying scripture while transcribing what the Holy Spirit reveals about my purpose. Throughout this book I found myself wondering how my own life would have been altered if I had crossed paths with Saint Francis or Saint Clare.

While I am no longer a Southern Baptist, I remain a Christian. I now attend a nondenominational church with a contemporary worship service complete with electric guitar and bongo drums. Sunday services overflow with praise music and waves of people raising their hands, swaying to the beat of the drums. What initially jarred the foundation of the traditional worship that I was accustomed to is the very thing that now draws me to church. Occasionally I find my own hands lifted high toward the One I seek to praise. I've come to learn that praising God is more than being satisfied and thankful when all is right in life. It's a sacrifice of praise even when life is not functioning properly—simply praising God because He is God. The writings of Saint Francis help me understand this concept. While reading The Canticle of Brother Sun, I found myself putting the words to music and suddenly realized how similar the words are to the contemporary songs that we sing in churches today. Perhaps Saint Francis was ahead of his time. Perhaps he too would have enjoyed the freedom of nontraditional worship. Now I can no longer walk outside and look up to the heavens without thinking of his writings. "Praised be You, my Lord, through Sister Moon and the stars; in heaven You formed them clear and precious and beautiful." Saint Francis reminds us that we first and foremost belong to God and that everything in our surroundings and in our lives are His and His alone. He allows us to experience His creation and perhaps even love one of His creatures, but in the end it all belongs to Him.

Saint Francis and Saint Clare truly did find God more desirable than all else. While reading about their lives and work, I was struck by Jesus's command to the rich man in Matt. 19. When a rich young man asks Jesus how he can be a follower, Jesus responds by saying: "If you want to be perfect, go, sell your possessions and give to the poor and you will have treasure in heaven. Then come, follow me." If we were really being honest, most of us would have to confess that we would have walked away saddened, like the rich man we find in scripture. "Give up our possessions, our social standing?" we would have asked Jesus—or at least we would have thought it. But Saint Francis and Saint Clare accepted Jesus's command and turned their backs on the wealth that had comforted them in their youth. By doing so, they endured hardship, family anger, and loss of friends. What they received were peace, miracles, and an eternal inheritance in Jesus Christ. Their example lives on.

—MICHAEL MORRIS

PART ONE

✳

The Writings of
Saint Francis

A BRIEF BIOGRAPHY OF FRANCIS OF ASSISI

Francis of Assisi (1181–1224) is one of the most popular saints in Christian history, known for his love of creation and of creatures. Stories are told of his affection for animals, especially how he tamed a wolf that was terrifying an Italian town. His spirituality as revealed in "Brother Sun" and "Sister Moon" suggests a deep affirmation of created things.

The son of a successful businessman in Assisi, Francis was a carouser in his youth, and became a soldier for Assisi in its rivalry with another Italian town. A high-spirited person of artistic temperament, he was engaged by pursuits of war and self-indulgence. He loved beautiful things, music, dancing and the arts.

But in 1206, when he was twenty-four, Francis experienced a conversion. He began to feel dissatisfied with what he previously had enjoyed. During parties and celebrations he felt alienated from the festive spirit. Repelled by disease and ugliness, he nevertheless felt drawn to associate with beggars, to seek out and care for lepers, and to take on works of charity.

After a few years of this ambivalence, Francis one day found himself walking in the country outside the gates of Assisi. As he passed the dilapidated church of San Damiano, he felt prompted to go in and pray. There, before a small Byzantine-style crucifix, Francis heard the Lord say, "Go and repair my house, which you see is falling down." Francis did repair that church. But his response to God's command went even further than that. On fire with devotion, and sensitive to the needs of the poor, Francis renounced his father's way of life, even his own clothes, and took up a religious calling, including voluntary poverty, prayer, and preaching. Adhering to the Gospel, he soon attracted a following of poor preachers who went far and wide in the service of Christ. He also traveled into Muslim-dominated lands in an effort to preach the message of Jesus Christ.

Francis was entirely governed by love of Christ (and Lady Poverty). He also exerted organizational leadership and wrote a Franciscan rule. The religious order he founded, sanctioned by the Roman Catholic Church, continues to have broad influence through communities both of men and of women.

Late in life, through intense prayer Francis received the stigmata, wounds resembling those of the crucified Christ. His life ended in blindness, botched surgery, and great physical pain. Franciscan spirituality gained enormous popularity in his lifetime and has never really lost ground. Francis continues to be one of the best known and most loved among all the saints.

1. The Canticle of Brother Sun

Song, music, and poetry were so deeply a part of the nature of Saint Francis that in times of sorrow and sickness as well as of joy and good health he spontaneously gave voice in song to his feelings, his inspirations, and his prayers. The clearest expression of this aspect of the personality of il Poverello—"the Poor Man of Assisi," as Saint Francis was known—is the Canticle of Brother Sun. G. K. Chesterton, in his reflections on the saint, wrote of this work: "It is a supremely characteristic work and much of Saint Francis could be reconstructed from that work alone."

This magnificent hymn expresses the mystical vision of Saint Francis of Assisi and, since it springs from the depths of his soul, provides us with many insights into the profundity of his life of faith in the triune God, who so deeply enters into creation. In this vision, however, the Poor Man does not lose himself in space or in the vastness of the created world. He becomes so intimate and familiar with the wonders of creation that he embraces them as "Brother" and "Sister"—that is, members of one family. More than any other aspect of the Canticle of Brother Sun, this unique feature has enhanced the spiritual tradition of Christian spirituality.

> Most high, all-powerful, good Lord,
> Yours are the praises, the glory, the honor, and all blessing.
> To You alone, Most High, do they belong,
> and no man is worthy to mention Your name.
> Praised be You, my Lord, with all your creatures,
> especially Sir Brother Sun,
> who is the day and through whom You give us light.
> And he is beautiful and radiant with great splendor;

and bears a likeness of You, most high One.

Praised be You, my Lord, through Sister Moon and the stars;

in heaven You formed them clear and precious and beautiful.

Praised be You, my Lord, through Brother Wind,

and through the air, cloudy and serene, and every kind
    of weather

through which You give sustenance to Your creatures.

Praised be You, my Lord, through Sister Water,

who is very useful and humble and precious and chaste.

Praised be You, my Lord, through Brother Fire,

through whom You light the night,

and he is beautiful and playful and robust and strong.

Praised be You, my Lord, through our Sister Mother Earth,

who sustains and governs us,

and who produces varied fruits with colored flowers and herbs.

Praised be You, my Lord, through those who give pardon
    for Your love

and bear infirmity and tribulation.

Blessed are those who endure in peace,

for by You, Most High, they shall be crowned.

Praised be You, my Lord, through our Sister Bodily Death,

from whom no living man can escape.

Woe to those who die in mortal sin.

Blessed are those whom death will find in Your most holy will,

for the second death shall do them no harm.

Praise and bless my Lord and give Him thanks

and serve Him with great humility.

2. The Canticle of Exhortation to Saint Clare and Her Sisters

The Legend of Perugia (a medieval account of Saint Francis and his work) mentions the composition of another canticle inspired by the need to console and encourage the Poor Ladies of San Damiano—that is, Saint Clare and her sisters (also later known as the Poor Clares). The text of this piece seemed to have been lost until 1941, when it was published with the Rule and Constitutions of the Nuns of the Order of Saint Clare. In 1976, however, Father Giovanni Boccali discovered a fourteenth-century manuscript in a convent of the Poor Clares in Verona, Italy, and in 1978 published his evidence for its authenticity. The text was written in the dialect of the Umbrian Valley and thus is closely associated with the Canticle of Brother Sun, which was composed in the same language.

Listen, little poor ones called by the Lord,
who have come together from many parts and provinces:
Live always in truth,
that you may die in obedience.
Do not look at the life outside,
for that of the Spirit is better.
I beg you through great love,
to use with discretion
the alms which the Lord gives you.
Those who are weighed down by sickness
and others who are wearied because of them,
all of you: bear it in peace.

For you will sell this fatigue at a very high price
and each one [of you] will be crowned queen
in heaven with the Virgin Mary.

3. The Exhortation to the Praise of God

The text of this prayer comes through a manuscript written by the Franciscan historian Marianus of Florence (d. 1537). The author claims that the prayer was written on a wooden panel that formed an antependium of an altar in the hermitage of Cesi di Terni in Umbria. Marianus and an anonymous scribe who copied the text concur that Saint Francis wrote some verses on the panel and had pictures of various creatures drawn on it. Unfortunately, the panel was lost after these witnesses brought attention to it, but its description provides a tool for understanding the contents of the prayer.

Fear the Lord and give Him honor.

The Lord is worthy to receive praise and honor.

All you who fear the Lord, praise Him.

Hail Mary, full of grace, the Lord is with you.

Heaven and earth, praise Him.

All you rivers, praise Him.

All you children of God, bless the Lord.

This is the day which the Lord has made; let us exult and
    rejoice in it!

Alleluia, alleluia, alleluia! O King of Israel!

Let every spirit praise the Lord.

Praise the Lord for He is good; all you who read this, bless
    the Lord.

All you creatures, bless the Lord.

All you birds of the heavens, praise the Lord.

All you children, praise the Lord.

Young men and virgins, praise the Lord.

The Lamb Who was slain is worthy to receive praise, glory, and honor.

Blessed be the holy Trinity and undivided Unity.

Saint Michael the Archangel, defend us in battle.

4. The Prayer before the Crucifix

The biographies of Saint Francis written by Thomas of Celano and Saint Bonaventure in the thirteenth century characterize the early years of the saint's conversion as a struggle to discern God's will. Both of these authors, as well as the author of The Legend of the Three Companions, describe the scene in the deserted Church of San Damiano in Assisi during which the young Francis heard a command of the crucified Lord while he was absorbed in prayer. "Francis," the voice told him, "go and repair My house, which, as you see, is falling completely into ruin." The remainder of his life was spent consciously or unconsciously responding to that command.

Almost all of the manuscripts that contain this simple prayer indicate its origin at the foot of the crucifix in the Church of San Damiano. It clearly reflects the struggle of the early years of the saint's life as well as his ever-present desire to fulfill the will of God. Thus it is a prayer that can be seen as characterizing il Poverello's entire life.

Most high,
glorious God,
enlighten the darkness of my heart
and give me, Lord,
a correct faith,
a certain hope,
a perfect charity,
sense and knowledge,
so that I may carry out Your holy and true command.

5. The Prayer Inspired by the Our Father

Both Thomas of Celano and Saint Bonaventure wrote of the lessons on prayer centered on the Our Father that Saint Francis gave to his friars. The Earlier Rule (page 13) verifies the saint's love of this simple Gospel prayer. Meditation on each phrase of the Our Father was quite common in the Middle Ages, as the writings of Saint Bernard of Clairvaux and Hugh of Saint Victor indicate. Recent scholarship has accepted the prayer below as authentic, though not original (because Saint Francis borrowed heavily from other writings). The scholars base their arguments on the presence of many biblical images and passages that are present in the other writings of the saint. In many ways, this Prayer Inspired by the Our Father is an expression of the inner life of Saint Francis.

O our most holy Father:
O our Creator, Redeemer, Consoler, and Savior
Who art in heaven:
In the angels and in the saints,
enlightening them to love, because You, Lord, are light
inflaming them to love, because You, Lord, are love
dwelling [in them] and filling them with happiness
because You, Lord, are the Supreme Good, the Eternal Good
from Whom comes all good
without Whom there is no good
Hallowed be Your name:
May our knowledge of You become ever clearer
That we may know the breadth of Your blessings
the length of Your promises

the height of Your majesty

the depth of Your judgments

Your kingdom come:

So that You may rule in us through Your grace

and enable us to come to Your kingdom,

where there is an unclouded vision of You

a perfect love of You

a blessed companionship with You

an eternal enjoyment of You

Your will be done on earth as it is in heaven:

That we may love You with our whole heart by always
  thinking of You

with our whole soul by always desiring You

with our whole mind by directing all our intentions to You
  and by seeking Your glory in everything

and with our whole strength by spending all our energies
  and affections of soul and body in the service of Your
  love and of nothing else

and may we love our neighbors as ourselves

by drawing them all with our whole strength to Your love

by rejoicing in the good fortunes of others as well as our own

by sympathizing with the misfortunes of others

and by giving offense to no one

Give us this day:

In memory and understanding and reverence

of the love which [our Lord Jesus Christ] had for us

and of those things which He said and did and suffered for us

Our daily bread:

Your own beloved Son, our Lord Jesus Christ

And forgive us our trespasses:

Through Your ineffable mercy

through the power of the Passion of Your beloved Son

together with the merits and intercession of the blessed

    Virgin Mary and all Your chosen ones

As we forgive those who trespass against us:

And whatever we do not forgive perfectly

do You, Lord, enable us to forgive to the full

so that we may truly love [our] enemies

and fervently intercede for them before You,

returning no one evil for evil

and striving to help everyone in You

And lead us not into temptation:

Hidden or obvious

sudden or persistent

But deliver us from evil:

Past, present, and to come

Glory to the Father and to the Son and to the Holy Spirit,

as it was in the beginning, is now, and will be forever.

    Amen.

6. The Earlier Rule

The development of the Rule of the Friars Minor is one of the areas of Franciscan research that has prompted the greatest attention throughout the centuries. (The rule of a religious order specifies how members of that order should live.) As long as the primitive fraternity was still small in number, the charismatic personality of Saint Francis substituted for the lack of precise regulations and specifications that would come in a longer rule. After the marvelous growth of the order—especially after 1217 and 1219, when the friars scaled the Alps and crossed the Mediterranean—it was necessary to provide new guidelines to maintain the ideals and enthusiasm of the primitive fraternity. The Earlier Rule (so named in retrospect because it was followed by the Later Rule) addressed that need. The hand of someone well versed in scripture, particularly the Synoptic Gospels, can be seen in this text. That person, according to the thirteenth-century chronicler Jordan of Giano, was Caesar of Speyer, whom Saint Francis asked to embellish the text of the rule with appropriate scriptural passages.

The Earlier Rule is one of the richest spiritual documents of the Franciscan tradition. It provides innumerable insights into the ideals of Saint Francis, as well as indications of the tensions and forces that shaped the brotherhood gathered around him.

Prologue

In the name of the Father and of the Son and of the Holy Spirit.

This is the life of the Gospel of Jesus Christ which Brother Francis asked the Lord Pope to be granted and confirmed for him; and he granted and confirmed it for him and his brothers present and to come. Brother Francis and whoever will be the head of this order promises obedience and reverence to the Lord Pope Innocent and to his successors. And all the other brothers are bound to obey Brother Francis and his successors.

Chapter I: Living without anything of one's own and in chastity and obedience

The rule and life of these brothers is this: to live in obedience, in chastity, and without anything of their own, and to follow the teaching and the footprints of our Lord Jesus Christ, Who says: If you wish to be perfect, go and sell everything you have and give it to the poor, and you will have treasure in heaven; and come, follow Me [Matt. 19:21; Luke 18:22]. And, If anyone wishes to come after Me, let him deny himself and take up his cross and follow Me [Matt. 16:24]. Again: If anyone wishes to come to Me and does not hate father and mother and wife and children and brothers and sisters, and even his own life, he cannot be My disciple [Luke 14:26]. And: Everyone who has left father or mother, brothers or sisters, wife or children, houses or lands because of Me, shall receive a hundredfold and shall possess eternal life [cf. Matt. 19:29; Mark 10:29; Luke 18:30].

Chapter II: The reception and the clothing of the brothers

If anyone, desiring by divine inspiration to accept this life, should come to our brothers, let him be received by them with kindness. And if he is determined to accept our life, the brothers should take great care not to become involved in his temporal affairs; but let them present him to their minister as quickly as possible. The minister on his part should receive him with kindness and encourage him and diligently explain to him the tenor of our life. When this has been done, the aforesaid person—if he wishes and is able to do so spiritually and without any impediment—should sell all his possessions and strive to give them all [the proceeds] to the poor. The brothers and the minister of the brothers should take care not to become involved in any way in his temporal affairs; nor should they accept any money either themselves or through an intermediary. However, if they are in need, the brothers can accept instead of money other things needed for the body, as other poor people do. And when he has returned, let the minister give him the clothes of probation for a whole year—namely, two tunics without a hood, a cord and trousers, and a small cape reaching to the cord. When the year and term of probation has ended, let him be received into obedience. Afterward he will not be allowed to join another order or to "wander outside obedience" according to the decree of the Lord Pope and according to the Gospel; for no one who puts his hand to the plow and looks back is fit for the kingdom of God [Luke 9:62].

But if someone should come who cannot give away his possessions without an impediment and yet has the spiritual desire [to do so], let him leave those things behind; and this suffices for him. No one should be accepted contrary to the form and the prescription of the holy Church. The other brothers who have already promised obedience should have one tunic with a hood and another without a hood, if that is necessary, and a cord and trousers. And all the brothers should wear poor clothes, and they can patch them with sackcloth and other pieces with the blessing of God; for the Lord says in the Gospel: Those who wear costly clothes and live in luxury [Luke 7:25] and who dress in soft garments are in the houses of kings [Matt. 11:8]. And although they may be called hypocrites, nonetheless they should not cease doing good nor should they seek costly clothing in this world, so that they may have a garment in the kingdom of heaven.

Chapter III: The divine office and fasting

The Lord says: This kind of devil cannot come out except by fasting and by prayer [Mark 9:28]; and again, When you fast do not become sad like the hypocrites [Matt. 6:16].

For this reason all the brothers, whether clerical or lay, should celebrate the Divine Office, the praises and prayers, as is required of them. The clerical [brothers] should celebrate the office and say it for the living and the dead according to the custom of the clergy. And for the failings and negligence of the brothers, they should say daily the Miserere mei, Deus (Psalm 50), with the Our Father; and for the deceased brothers let them say the De profundis (Psalm 129) with the Our Father. And they may have only the books necessary to fulfill their office. And the lay [brothers] who know how to read the Psalter may have it. But those who do not know how to read should not have any book. The lay [brothers] should say the I Believe in God and twenty-four Our Fathers with the Glory to the Father for Matins; for Lauds, they should say five;

for Prime, the I Believe in God and seven Our Fathers with the Glory to the Father; for each of the hours—Terce, Sext, and None—seven; for Vespers, twelve; for Compline, the I Believe in God and seven Our Fathers with the Glory to the Father; for the deceased [brothers], seven Our Fathers with the Eternal Rest; and for the failings and negligence of the brothers three Our Fathers every day.

Similarly, all the brothers should fast from the Feast of All Saints until Christmas, and from the Epiphany, when our Lord Jesus Christ began to fast, until Easter. At other times, however, they are not obliged to fast according to this life except on Fridays. And they may eat whatever food is placed before them, according to the Gospel.

Chapter IV: The ministers and the other brothers

In the name of the Lord. All the brothers who have been established as ministers and servants of the other brothers should assign their brothers to the provinces and to the places where they are to be, and they should visit them frequently and spiritually admonish and encourage them. And all my other blessed brothers should diligently obey them in those matters which concern the well-being of their soul and [which] are not contrary to our life. And among themselves let them behave according to what the Lord says: Whatever you wish that men should do to you, do that to them [Matt. 7:12]; and, That which you do not wish to be done to you, do not do to another [Tob. 4:16]. And let the ministers and servants remember what the Lord says:

I have come not to be served, but to serve [Matt. 20:28]; and because the care of the souls of the brothers has been entrusted to them, if any one of them should be lost because of their fault or bad example, [these ministers and servants] will have to render an account before the Lord Jesus Christ on the day of judgment [cf. Matt. 12:36].

Chapter V: The correction of brothers who are at fault

Therefore, guard your soul and those of your brothers, since it is a terrible thing to fall into the hands of the living God. But should any of the ministers command any of the brothers to do something contrary to our life or against his conscience, he is not bound to obey him, since that is not obedience in which a fault or sin is committed. Nonetheless, all the brothers, who are subject to the ministers and servants, should reasonably and diligently consider the actions of the ministers and servants. And if they should see that any of them is living according to the flesh and not according to the Spirit—[as demanded] for the integrity of our life—if he does not amend his way, after a third admonition they should inform the minister and servant of the whole fraternity at the Chapter of Pentecost without any interference or opposition. If, moreover, among the brothers anywhere there should be some brother who wishes to live according to the flesh and not according to the Spirit, the brothers with whom he is [living] should admonish, instruct, and correct him humbly and diligently. But if, after the third admonition, he should refuse to change his ways, as soon as they can they should send him or report him to their minister and servant, and the minister and servant should deal with him as he considers best before God.

And let all the brothers, both the ministers and servants as well as the others, take care not to be disturbed or angered at the sin or the evil of another, because the devil wishes to destroy many through the fault of one; but they should spiritually help [the brother] who has sinned as best they can, because it is not the healthy who are in need of the physician, but those who are sick.

Similarly, all the brothers in this regard should not hold power or dominion, least of all among themselves. For, as the Lord says in the Gospel: The rulers of the peoples have power over them, and their leaders rule over them [Matt. 20:25]; it shall not be like this among the brothers. And whoever among them wishes to become the greater should be their minister and servant. And whoever is the greater among them should become like the lesser.

Nor should any brother do evil or say something evil to another; on the contrary, through the charity of the Spirit, they should voluntarily serve and obey one another. And this is the true and holy obedience of our Lord Jesus Christ. And all the brothers, as often as they have turned away from the commands of the Lord and wandered outside obedience, as the prophet says [Ps. 118:21], should know that they are cursed outside obedience as long as they knowingly persist in such sin. And when they have persevered in the commands of the Lord, which they have promised through the holy Gospel and their life, they should know that they are standing firm in true obedience and that they are blessed by the Lord.

Chapter VI: The recourse of the brothers to the minister; calling no brother prior

If the brothers, in whatever places they are, cannot observe our life, they should have recourse as quickly as possible to their minister and report this to him. The minister, on his part, should be eager to provide for them as he would wish to be done for him were he in a similar position. And no one should be called prior, but all generally should be called Friars Minor. And the one should wash the feet of the others.

Chapter VII: The manner of serving and working

None of the brothers should be administrators or managers in whatever places they are staying among others to serve or to work, nor should they be supervisors in the houses in which they serve, nor should they accept any office which might generate scandal or be harmful to their souls; instead, they should be the lesser ones and subject to all who are in the same house.

And the brothers who know how to work should do so and should exercise that trade which they [already] know, if it is not against the good of the soul and can be performed honestly. For the prophet says: You shall eat the fruits of your labors; you are blessed and it will be well for you [Ps. 127:2]. And the Apostle [Paul says]: Whoever does not wish to work shall not eat [cf. 2 Thess. 3:10]; and, Everyone should remain in that skill and office in which he has been called [1 Cor. 7:24]. And they may receive for their work everything necessary except money. And when it should be necessary, let them seek alms like other poor people. And they may have the tools and instruments suitable for their trades.

All the brothers should always be intent on good works, for it is written [by Saint Gregory]: "Always do something good so that the devil will find you occupied." And again [by Saint Benedict]: "Idleness is the enemy of the soul." Therefore, the servants of God must always give themselves totally to prayer or to some good work.

The brothers should beware that, whether they are in hermitages or in other places, they do not make any place their own or contend with anyone about it. And whoever comes to them, friend or foe, thief or robber, should be received with kindness. And wherever the brothers are and in whatever place they meet other brothers, they must greet one another wholeheartedly and lovingly and honor one another without complaining. And they must beware not to appear outwardly sad and like gloomy hypocrites; but let them show that they are joyful in the Lord and cheerful and truly gracious.

Chapter VIII: The brothers not receiving money

The Lord commands us in the Gospel: Watch, be on your guard against all malice and greed [cf. Luke 12:15]. Guard yourselves against the preoccupations of this world and the cares of this life [cf. Luke 21:34].

Therefore, none of the brothers, wherever he may be or wherever he goes, should in any way carry, receive, or have received [by another] either money or coins, whether for clothing or for books or for payment for any work—indeed, for no reason—unless it is for the evident need of the sick brothers; for we must not suppose that money or coins have any greater value than stones. And the devil would like to blind those who desire it or consider it better than stones. Therefore, let us who have left all things behind take care that we do not lose the kingdom of heaven for so little. And if we were to find coins in any place, let us give them no more thought than the dust which we crush with our feet; for all [this is] vanity of vanities, and all is vanity. And if by chance—which God forbid—it should happen that some brother has collected or is hoarding money or coins, with the sole exception of the needs of the sick as mentioned above, all the brothers are to consider him as a false brother and an apostate, and a thief and a robber, and as the one who held the purse, unless he has truly repented.

And in no way may the brothers receive [money] or arrange to have it received, or beg money or arrange to have it sought as alms or coins for any houses or places; and they may not go with a person who is begging money or coins for such places. But the brothers may perform for these places other services which are not contrary to our life, with the blessing of God. Nevertheless, at times of the evident necessity of the lepers the brothers can beg alms for them. Nonetheless, they should beware of money. Likewise, all the brothers should beware of running around the world for filthy gain.

Chapter IX: Begging alms

All the brothers should strive to follow the humility and the poverty of our Lord Jesus Christ and remember that we should have nothing else in the whole world except, as the Apostle says, something to eat and something to wear; we should be content with these [cf. 1 Tim. 6:8]. And they must rejoice when they live among people [who are considered to be] of little worth and who are looked down upon—among the poor and the powerless, the sick and the lepers, and the beggars by the wayside. And when it may be necessary, let them go for alms. And they should not be ashamed, but rather recall that our Lord Jesus Christ, the Son of the living and all-powerful God, set His face like flint and was not ashamed. And He was a poor man and a transient and lived on alms, He and the blessed Virgin, and His disciples. And should people shame them and refuse to give them alms, let them give thanks to God for this, since from such insults they will receive great honor before the tribunal of our Lord Jesus Christ. And let them know that such shame is credited not to those who suffer it but to those who caused it. And alms are a legacy and a just right due to the poor, which our Lord Jesus Christ acquired for us. And the brothers who labor to acquire them will receive a great reward and [at the same time] enable those who give [such alms] to gain and acquire [that reward] in return, for everything that people leave behind in the world will perish, but for the charity and the almsgiving which they have done they will receive a reward from the Lord.

And each one should confidently make known his need to the other, so that one brother might find what another needs and minister it to him. And each one should love and care for his brother in all those things in which God will give him grace, as a mother loves and cares for her son. And he who does not eat should not judge the one who does.

And whenever necessity should come upon them, all the brothers, wherever they may be, may eat all foods which people can eat, as the Lord says of David who ate the loaves of proposition which no one was permitted to eat except the priests [Mark 2:26]. And let them recall what the Lord says: Be on your guard that your hearts do not become bloated with self-indulgence and drunkenness and the cares of this life, for that day will come upon you unexpectedly; for like a trap it will come upon all who dwell upon the face of the earth [Luke 21:34–35]. Likewise, even in times of manifest necessity, all the brothers should take care of their needs, as the Lord gives them the grace, since "necessity knows no law."

Chapter X: The sick brothers

If any of the brothers shall fall ill, wherever he may be, the other brothers should not leave him behind unless one of the brothers, or several of them if that be necessary, is assigned to serve him as that brother would wish to be served himself; but in case of grave necessity, they can entrust him to some person capable of taking care of him in his illness. And I beg the sick brother to give thanks to the Creator for everything; and whatever the Lord wills for him, he should desire to be that, whether healthy or sick, since all those whom God has predestined for everlasting life He instructs by means of the afflictions of punishment and sickness and the spirit of repentance. As the Lord says: I correct and punish those whom I love [Rev. 3:19].

And if anyone should be disturbed or become angry at God or at [his] brothers, or if by chance he persistently asks for medicines with a great desire to free the flesh which is soon to die and is the enemy of the soul, [remember:] All this comes from the evil one. [Such a person] is totally caught up with the flesh and does not seem to be one of the brothers, since he loves his body more than his soul.

Chapter XI: Loving one another without blasphemy or detraction

And all the brothers should beware that they do not slander or engage in disputes; rather, they should strive to keep silence whenever God gives them [this] grace. Nor should they quarrel among themselves or with others, but they should strive to respond humbly, saying: I am a useless servant. And they should not become angry, since everyone who grows angry with his brother shall be liable to judgment; and he who has said to his brother "fool" shall be liable to the Council; whoever has said "idiot" shall be liable to the fires of hell. And they should love one another, as the Lord says: This is My commandment: that you love one another as I have loved you [John 15:12]. And let them express the love which they have for one another by their deeds, as the Apostle says: Let us not love in word or speech, but in deed and in truth [1 John 3:18]. And they should slander no one. Let them not murmur nor detract from others, for it is written: Gossips and detractors are detestable to God [Rom. 1:29–30]. And let them be modest, by showing meekness toward everyone. Let them not judge or condemn. And as the Lord says, they should not take notice of the little defects of others [cf. Matt. 7:3; Luke 6:41]. Rather they should reflect much more on their own [sins] in the bitterness of their soul. And let them strive to enter through the narrow gate, for the Lord says: Narrow is the gate and hard the road that leads to life; and there are few who find it [Matt. 7:14].

Chapter XII: Impure glances and frequent association with women

All the brothers, wherever they are or go, should avoid impure glances and association with women. And no one should counsel women or travel alone [with them] or eat at table [with them] from the same plate. The priests should speak honorably with them when giving them [the sacrament of] penance or some spiritual advice. And absolutely no woman should be received to obedience by any brothers, but once she has been given spiritual advice, let her perform a penance where she will. And all of us must keep close watch over ourselves and keep all parts of our body pure, since the Lord says: Anyone who looks lustfully at a woman has already committed adultery with her in his heart [Matt. 5:28]; and the Apostle says: Do you not know that your members are the temple of the Holy Spirit? [cf. 1 Cor. 6:19]; therefore, whoever violates God's temple, God will destroy him [1 Cor. 3:17].

Chapter XIII: The avoidance of fornication

If any brother, at the instigation of the devil, commits a sin of fornication, he should be deprived of the habit, which he has lost through his wickedness, and he should put it aside completely, and be totally expelled from our order. And afterward let him do penance for his sins.

Chapter XIV: The manner of the brothers' conduct in the world

When the brothers go about through the world, they should carry nothing for the journey—neither a knapsack, nor a purse, nor bread, nor money, nor a staff. And into whatever house they enter, let them first say: Peace to this house. And, remaining in that house, they may eat and drink whatever [their hosts] have offered. They should not offer resistance to evil, but if someone should strike them on one cheek, let them offer him the other as well. And if someone should take away their clothes, they should not deny him also their tunic. They should give to all who ask; and if anyone takes what is theirs, they should not demand that it be returned.

Chapter XV: Against riding horses

I enjoin upon all my brothers both cleric and lay that, when they go through the world or stay in places, they should in no way have any animal either with themselves or in the care of another or in any other way. Nor may they ride horses unless they are compelled by sickness or great necessity.

Chapter XVI: Those who are going among the Saracens and other nonbelievers

The Lord says: Behold, I am sending you as lambs in the midst of wolves. Therefore, be prudent as serpents and simple as doves [Matt. 10:16]. Therefore, any brother who, by divine inspiration, desires to go among the Saracens and other nonbelievers should go with the permission of his minister and servant. And the minister should give [these brothers] permission and not oppose them, if he shall see that they are fit to be sent; for he shall be bound to give an account to the Lord if he has proceeded without discretion in this or in other matters. As for the brothers who go, they can live spiritually among [the Saracens and nonbelievers] in two ways. One way is not to engage in arguments or disputes, but to be subject to every human creature for God's sake and to acknowledge that they are Christians. Another way is to proclaim the word of God when they see that it pleases the Lord, so that they believe in the all-powerful God—Father, and Son, and Holy Spirit—the Creator of all, in the Son Who is the Redeemer and Savior, and that they be baptized and become Christians; because whoever has not been born again of water and the Holy Spirit cannot enter into the kingdom of God.

They can say to [the Saracens] and to others these and other things which will have pleased the Lord, for the Lord says in the Gospel: Everyone who acknowledge Me before men I will also acknowledge before My Father Who is in heaven [Matt. 10:32]. And: Whoever is ashamed of Me and My words, the Son of Man will also be ashamed of him when He comes in His majesty and that of the Father and the angels [Luke 9:26].

And all the brothers, wherever they may be, should remember that they gave themselves and abandoned their bodies to the Lord Jesus Christ. And for love of Him, they must make themselves vulnerable to their enemies, both visible and invisible, because the Lord says: Whoever loses his life for My sake will save it in eternal life [Matt. 25:46]. Blessed are those who suffer persecution for the sake of justice, for the kingdom of heaven is theirs [Matt. 5:10]. If they have persecuted Me, they will also persecute you [John 15:20]. And: If they persecute you in one city, flee to another. Blessed are you when people shall hate you and malign and persecute you and drive you out, abuse you, denounce your name as evil [Luke 6:22], and utter every kind of slander against you because of Me [Matt. 5:11]. Rejoice on that day and be glad [Luke 6:23], because your reward is very great in heaven. And [the Lord says]: I say to you, my friends, do not be frightened by these things [Luke 12:4] and do not fear those who kill the body [Matt. 10:28] and after that can do no more [Luke 12:4]. Take care not to be disturbed [Matt. 24:6]. For through your patience, you will possess your souls [Luke 21:19]; and whoever perseveres to the end will be saved [Matt. 10:22; 24:13].

Chapter XVII: Preachers

No brother should preach contrary to the form and regulations of the holy Church nor unless he has been permitted by his minister. And the minister should take care not to grant [this permission] to anyone indiscriminately. All the brothers, however, should preach by their deeds. And no minister or preacher should appropriate to himself the ministry of the brothers or the office of preaching, but he should set it aside without any protest whenever he is told.

Therefore, in the love which is God, I beg all my brothers—those who preach, pray, or work, whether cleric or lay—to strive to humble themselves in all things [and] not to take pride in themselves or to delight in themselves or be puffed up interiorly about their good works and deeds—in fact, about any good thing that God does or says or sometimes works in them and through them. [This is] in keeping with what the Lord says: Yet do not rejoice in this: that the spirits are subject to you [Luke 10:20]. And we should be firmly convinced that nothing belongs to us except [our] vices and sins. Rather, we must rejoice when we would fall into various trials and endure every sort of anguish of soul and body or ordeals in this world for the sake of eternal life.

Therefore, all [of us] brothers must beware of all pride and vainglory. And let us keep ourselves from the wisdom of this world and the prudence of the flesh. For the spirit of the flesh desires and is most eager to have words, but [cares] little to carry them out. And it does not seek a religion and holiness in the interior spirit, but it wishes and desires to have a religion and holiness outwardly apparent to people. And these are the ones of whom the Lord says: Truly I say to you: They have received their reward [Matt. 6:2]. But the Spirit of the Lord wishes the flesh to be mortified and despised, worthless and rejected. And it strives for humility and patience, and the pure and simple and true peace of the spiritual person. And above all things it always longs for the divine fear and the divine wisdom and the divine love of the Father, and of the Son, and of the Holy Spirit.

And let us refer all good to the most high and supreme
    Lord God,
and acknowledge that every good is His,
and thank Him for everything, [He] from Whom all good
    things come.
And may He,
the Highest and Supreme,
Who alone is true God,
have and be given and receive
every honor and reverence,
every praise and blessing,
every thanks and glory,
for every good is His,
He Who alone is good.

And when we see or hear an evil [person] speak, act, or blaspheme
God, let us speak well, act well, and praise God, Who is blessed forever.

Chapter XVIII: How the ministers meet together

Once a year each minister can come together with his brothers,
wherever they wish, on the Feast of Saint Michael the Archangel,
to treat of the things which refer to God. All the ministers who
are in those parts which are overseas and beyond the Alps may
come together once every three years, and the other ministers
once each year, to the Chapter of Pentecost at the Church of Saint
Mary of the Portiuncula, unless it has been decided otherwise by
the minister and servant of the entire fraternity.

Chapter XIX: The brothers living as Catholics

All the brothers must be Catholics [and] live and speak in a Catholic manner. But if any of them has strayed from the Catholic faith and life, in word or in deed, and has not amended his ways, he should be completely expelled from our fraternity. And we should regard all clerics and all religious who have not deviated from our religion as our lord in those things which pertain to the salvation of the soul, and, in the Lord, we should respect their order and their office and government.

Chapter XX: Penance and the reception of the body and blood of our Lord Jesus Christ

And my blessed brothers, both the clerics as well as the lay, should confess their sins to priests of our order. And if they should not be able to do so, they should confess to other prudent and Catholic priests, knowing full well that when they have received penance and absolution from any Catholic priests, they are without doubt absolved from their sins, provided they have humbly and faithfully fulfilled the penance imposed upon them. But if they have not been able to find a priest, they may confess to their brother, as the Apostle James says: Confess your sins to one another [James 5:16]. Despite this let them not fail to have recourse to a priest, since the power of binding and loosing is granted only to priests. And thus contrite and confessed, they should receive the body and blood of our Lord Jesus Christ with great humility and reverence, remembering what the Lord says: Whoever eats My flesh and drinks My blood has eternal life [cf. John 6:55]; and, Do this in memory of Me [Luke 22:19].

Chapter XXI: The praise and exhortation which all the brothers can offer

And whenever it may please them, all my brothers can proclaim this or a like exhortation and praise among all the people with the blessing of God:

> Fear and honor, praise and bless, give thanks and adore
> the Lord God Almighty in Trinity and in Unity,
> the Father and the Son and the Holy Spirit
> the Creator of all.
> Do penance, performing worthy fruits of penance,
> since we will soon die.
> Give and it shall be given to you.
> Forgive, and you shall be forgiven.
> And if you do not forgive men their sins,
> the Lord will not forgive you your sins.
> Confess all your sins.
> Blessed are those who die in penance,
> for they shall be in the kingdom of heaven.
> Woe to those who do not die in penance,
> for they shall be the children of the devil, whose works
>   they do,
> and they shall go into the eternal fire.
> Beware and abstain from every evil and persevere in good
>   till the end.

Chapter XXII: An admonition to the brothers

Let us pay attention, all [my] brothers, to what the Lord says: Love your enemies and do good to those who hate you [cf. Matt. 5:44], for our Lord Jesus Christ, Whose footprints we must follow, called His betrayer "friend" [cf. Matt. 26:50] and gave Himself willingly to those who crucified Him. Our friends, then, are all those who unjustly afflict upon us trials and ordeals, shame and injuries, sorrows and torments, martyrdom and death; we must love them greatly, for we will possess eternal life because of what they bring upon us.

And we must hate our body with its vices and sins, because, by [our] living according to the flesh, the devil wishes to take from us the love of Jesus Christ and eternal life and to lose himself with everyone in hell. For through our own fault we are rotten, miserable, and opposed to good, but prompt and willing to [embrace] evil, for as our Lord says in the Gospel: From the heart of man come forth and flow evil thoughts, adulteries, fornications, murders, thefts, avarice, wantonness, deceit, lewdness, evil looks, false testimonies, blasphemy, foolishness [cf. Mark 7:21–22; Matt. 15:19]; all these evil things flow from within, from the heart of a person, and these are the things that make a person unclean [Matt.15:20].

And now that we have left the world, we have nothing else to do except to follow the will of the Lord and to please Him. Let us take great care not to be earth along the wayside, or among the rocks, or among thorns. As the Lord says in the Gospel: The seed is the word of God [Luke 8:11ff.].

But that which fell along the wayside and was trampled under-
foot are those who hear the word and do not understand it. And
immediately the devil comes and snatches up what was planted
in their hearts and takes the word out of their hearts, otherwise
believing they might be saved.

But that which fell upon stony ground are those who, once
they have heard the word, at the outset receive it with joy. But
when tribulation and persecution overtake them because of the
word, they falter at once and they have no roots in them, but last
only for a time, because they believe for a time and in time of
temptation they fail.

That which fell among thorns are those who hear the word of
God, yet anxiety and the worries of this world and the lure of riches
and other inordinate desires come in to choke the word, and they
remain without fruit.

But that which is sown on good soil are those who hear the
word with a good and noble heart and understand it and keep it
and bear fruit in patience.

And so we brothers, as the Lord says, should leave the dead to
bury their own dead [Matt. 8:22].

And let us be very careful of the malice and the subtlety of
Satan, who wishes that a man not raise his mind and heart to
God. And as he roams about he wishes to ensnare the heart of a
person under the guise of some reward or help, and to snuff out
our memory of the word and the precepts of the Lord, and
wishes to blind the heart of a person through worldly affairs and
concerns, and to live there. As the Lord says: When an unclean

spirit has gone out of a person, it wanders through dry and
waterless places seeking rest; and not finding any, says: I will
return to the house which I left [Luke 11:24]. And coming to it,
it finds it empty, swept, clean, and tidied [Matt. 12:44]. And it
goes off and brings seven other spirits more wicked than itself,
and they go in and live there. And the last condition of the person
is worst than the first.

Therefore, all [my] brothers, let us be very much on our guard
so that we do not lose or turn away our mind and heart from the
Lord under the guise of [achieving] some reward or [doing]
some work or [providing] some help. But in the holy love which
is God, I beg all [my] brothers, both the ministers and the others,
as they overcome every obstacle and put aside every care and anxiety, to strive as best they can to serve, love, honor, and adore the
Lord God with a clean heart and a pure mind, for this is what He
desires above all things.

And let us make a home and dwelling place for Him Who is the
Lord God Almighty, Father and Son and Holy Spirit, Who says:
Watch, therefore, praying constantly that you may be considered
worthy to escape all the evils that are to come and to stand secure
before the Son of Man [Luke 21:36]. And when you stand to pray
say: Our Father Who art in heaven [Matt. 6:9]. And let us adore
Him with a pure heart, because we should pray always and not
lose heart; for the Father seeks such worshippers. God is Spirit, and
those who worship Him must worship Him in spirit and in truth.

And let us have recourse to Him as to the shepherd and
guardian of our souls, Who says: I am the good shepherd who

feeds My sheep, and I lay down My life for My sheep. All of you are brothers. And do not call anyone on earth your father, for one is your Father, the One in heaven. And do not let yourselves be called teachers, for your teacher is the One Who is in heaven [cf. Matt. 23:8–10]. If you remain in Me, and My words remain in you, you may ask whatever you will and it will be done for you [John 15:7]. Wherever two or three are gathered together in My name, I am there in the midst of them [Matt. 18:20]. Behold I am with you until the consummation of the world [Matt. 28:20]. The words which I have spoken to you are spirit and life [John 6:64]. I am the way, the truth, and the life [John 14:6].

Let us, therefore, hold onto the words, the life, and the teaching and the holy Gospel of Him Who humbled Himself to ask His Father for us and to make His name known to us, saying: Father, glorify Your name and glorify Your Son so that Your Son may glorify You [John 17:1b]. Father, I have made Your name known to the men whom You have given to Me [John 17:6]. The words which You have given to Me I have given to them; and they have accepted them and know truly that I came from You, and have believed that You sent Me [John 17:8].

I pray for them—not for the world, but for those whom You have given Me—because they belong to You and all I have is Yours [John 17:9–10]. Holy Father, protect those in Your name whom You have given to Me, so that they may be one as We are [John 17:11b]. I say these things while still in the world, that they may have joy within them. I gave them Your word; and the world hated them because they do not belong to the world just as I do not belong to the world. I am not asking that You remove them from the world, but that You protect them from the evil one [John 17:14b–15].

Sanctify them in the truth. Your word is truth. As You have sent Me into the world, so I have sent them into the world. And for their sake I sanctify Myself, so that they may be sanctified in truth [John 17:17–19].

I pray not only for these, but also for those who because of their words will believe in Me, so that they may be completely one, and the world may know that You have sent Me and that You have loved them as You have loved Me [cf. John 17:17–23]. And I shall make Your name known to them, so that the love with which You have loved Me may be in them and I may be in them [cf. John 17:26]. Father, I wish that where I am those whom You have given Me may be with Me, so that they may see Your glory in Your Kingdom [Matt. 20:21]. Amen.

Chapter XXIII: Prayer and thanksgiving

All-powerful, most holy, most high and supreme God
Holy and just Father
Lord, King of heaven and earth
we thank You for Yourself
for through Your holy will
and through Your only Son
with the Holy Spirit
You have created all things spiritual and corporal

and, having made us in Your own image and likeness,
You placed us in paradise.
And through our own fault we have fallen.
And we thank You
for as through Your Son You created us
so also through Your holy love, with which You loved us,
You brought about His birth
as true God and true man
by the glorious, ever-virgin, most blessed, holy Mary
and You willed to redeem us captives
through His cross and blood and death.
And we thank You
for Your Son Himself will come again
in the glory of His majesty
to send the wicked ones
who have not done penance and who have not known You
into the eternal fire,
and to say to all those who have known You and have
    adored You
and have served You in penance:
"Come, you blessed of My Father,
receive the kingdom,
which has been prepared for you
from the beginning of the world."
And because all of us wretches and sinners
are not worthy to pronounce Your name,
we humbly ask that our Lord Jesus Christ

Your beloved Son, in whom You were well pleased,
together with the Holy Spirit, the Paraclete,
give You thanks as it pleases You and Him for everything,
[He] Who always satisfies You in everything
through Whom You have done such great things for us.
Alleluia!
And through Your love we humbly beg
the glorious Mother, most blessed Mary ever-virgin,
blessed Michael, Gabriel, and Raphael
and all the blessed choirs of seraphim, cherubim, thrones,
    dominations, principalities, powers, virtues, angels,
    archangels,
blessed John the Baptist,
John the Evangelist,
Peter, Paul,
and the blessed patriarchs, prophets,
the innocents, apostles, evangelists, disciples, martyrs,
    confessors, virgins,
the blessed Elijah and Henoch,
and all the saints who were, who will be, and who are
to give You thanks for these things as it pleases You,
the supreme and true God
eternal and living
with Your most beloved Son, our Lord Jesus Christ,
and the Holy Spirit, the Paraclete,
world without end.
    Amen. Alleluia.

And all of us lesser brothers, useless servants, humbly ask and beg all those who wish to serve the Lord God within the holy, catholic, and apostolic church, and all the following orders: priests, deacons, subdeacons, acolytes, exorcists, lectors, porters, and all clerics, all religious men and all religious women, all lay brothers and youths, the poor and the needy, kings and princes, workers and farmers, servants and masters, all virgins and continent and married women, all laypeople, men and women, all children, adolescents, the young and the old, the healthy and the sick, all the small and the great, all peoples, races, tribes, and tongues, all nations and all peoples everywhere on earth who are and who will be—that all of us may persevere in the true faith and in penance, for otherwise no one will be saved.

Let us all love the Lord God with all [our] heart, all [our] soul, all [our] mind, and all [our] strength [cf. Mark 12:30], with fortitude and with total understanding, with all of our powers, and with every effort, every affection, every emotion, every desire, and every wish. He has given and gives to each one of us [our] whole body, [our] whole soul, and [our] whole life. He created us and redeemed us, and will save us by His mercy alone. He did and does every good thing for us [who are] miserable and wretched, rotten and foul-smelling, ungrateful and evil.

Therefore
let us desire nothing else
let us wish for nothing else
let nothing else please us and cause us delight

except our Creator and Redeemer and Savior,
the one true God,
Who is the fullness of Good
all good, every good, the true and supreme good
Who alone is good
merciful and gentle
delectable and sweet
Who alone is holy
just and true
holy and right
Who alone is kind
innocent
pure
from Whom and through Whom and in Whom is
all pardon
all grace
all glory
of all the penitent and the just
of all the blessed who rejoice together in heaven.
Therefore
let nothing hinder us
nothing separate us
or nothing come between us.
Let all of us
wherever we are
in every place
at every hour

at every time of day
everyday and continually
believe truly and humbly
and keep in [our] heart and love, honor, adore, serve
praise and bless
glorify and exalt
magnify and give thanks to
the most high and supreme eternal God
Trinity and Unity
the Father and the Son and the Holy Spirit
Creator of all
Savior of all who believe in Him
and hope in Him
and love Him
Who is
without beginning and without end
unchangeable, invisible,
indescribable, ineffable,
incomprehensible, unfathomable,
blessed, worthy of praise,
glorious, exalted on high, sublime,
most high, gentle, lovable,
delectable and totally desirable above all else
forever.
    Amen.

Chapter XXIV: Conclusion

In the name of the Lord! I ask all the brothers to learn the tenor and sense of these things which have been written in this life for the salvation of our souls, and to call them frequently to mind. And I ask God that He Who is all-powerful, Three and One, bless all those who teach, learn, retain, remember, and put into practice all these things, each time they repeat and perform what has been written here for the salvation of our soul, and, kissing their feet, to love deeply, to guard and cherish [them]. And on behalf of Almighty God and the Lord Pope and by obedience, I, Brother Francis, firmly command and decree that no one remove anything from what has been written in this rule or make any written addition to these things; nor should the brothers have any other rule.

Glory to the Father and to the Son and to the Holy Spirit,
as it was in the beginning, is now, and will be forever.
Amen.

7. The Later Rule

The fundamental charter and form of life for the Order of Friars Minor is known as the Later Rule, which received papal approval on November 29, 1223. This simple document, which Thomas of Celano in his Second Life of Saint Francis called "the marrow of the Gospel," has become the foundation of the three "families" of the First Order of Saint Francis—that is, the Friars Minor, the Friars Minor Conventual, and the Friars Minor Capuchin. Moreover, the Later Rule is an expression of the deep bond of unity that firmly establishes the life of the order within that of the Catholic Church.

When the Later Rule is studied against the background of the Earlier Rule, its marvelous vision of the Gospel life comes into focus. This is a pattern or form of life that is meant to be lived in the pursuit of the Gospel mission—that is, in striving to witness and proclaim the mystery of the incarnate Word of God. At the very heart of this document, Saint Francis articulates the dynamism or the fundamental principle of the spiritual life: "the Spirit of the Lord and His holy manner of working." Thus he provides for his followers an important tool for understanding the totality of his vision.

Chapter I: The life of the Friars Minor begins

The rule and life of the Friars Minor is this: to observe the holy Gospel of our Lord Jesus Christ by living in obedience, without anything of their own, and in chastity. Brother Francis promises obedience and reverence to the Lord Pope Honorius and his canonically elected successors and to the Roman Church. And let the other brothers be bound to obey Brother Francis and his successors.

Chapter II: Those who wish to embrace this life and how they should be received

If there are any who wish to accept this life and come to our brothers, let them send them to the ministers provincial, to whom and to no other is permission granted for receiving brothers. The ministers should diligently examine them concerning the Catholic faith and the sacraments of the Church. And if they believe all these things and are willing to profess them faithfully and observe them steadfastly to the end; and [if] they have no wives, or if they have wives [who] have already taken a vow of continence and are of such an age that suspicion cannot be raised about them, [and who] have already entered a monastery or have given their husbands permission by the authority of the bishop of the diocese, let the ministers speak to them the words of the holy Gospel that they should go and sell all that belongs to them and strive to give it to the poor. If they cannot do this, their good will suffices. And let the brothers and their ministers beware not to become solicitous over their temporal affairs, so that they may freely dispose of their goods as the Lord may inspire them. But if they stand in need of counsel, the ministers may have permission to send them to some God-fearing persons who may advise them how they should give what they have to the poor. Then they may be given the clothes of probation—namely, two tunics without a hood, a cord, short trousers, and a little cape reaching to the cord, unless at some time it seems [proper] to these same ministers before God to make other provisions. When the year of probation is ended, let them be received into obedience, whereby they promise to observe this life and rule always. And in no way shall it be lawful for them to leave this order, according to the decree of the Lord Pope, since, according to the Gospel: No one having put his hand to the plow and looking back is fit for the kingdom of God [Luke 9:62]. And those who have already promised obedience may have one tunic with a hood and, if they wish, another without a hood. And those who are forced by necessity may wear shoes. And let all the brothers wear poor clothes, and let them mend them with pieces of sackcloth or other material, with the blessing of God. I admonish and exhort them not to look down or pass judgment on those people whom they see wearing soft and colorful clothing and enjoying the choicest food and drink; instead, each must criticize and despise himself.

Chapter III: The Divine Office; fasting; the way the brothers should go about the world

The clerical [brothers] shall celebrate the Divine Office according to the rite of the holy Roman Church, except for the Psalter, for which reason they may have breviaries. The lay [brothers], however, shall pray twenty-four Our Fathers for Matins, five for Lauds, seven for each of the hours of Prime, Terce, Sext, and None, twelve for Vespers, and seven for Compline. And they shall pray for the dead. And [all the brothers] shall fast from the Feast of All Saints until the Nativity of the Lord. May those who fast voluntarily for that holy Lent which begins at Epiphany and continues for forty days, which the Lord consecrated by His own fast, be blessed by the Lord; and those who do not wish to keep it shall not be obliged. But they shall fast during that other Lent which lasts until the Resurrection. At other times, however, they are not bound to fast except on Fridays. But in times of manifest necessity the brothers are not obliged to corporal fasting.

I counsel, admonish, and exhort my brothers in the Lord Jesus Christ that, when they go about the world, they do not quarrel or fight with words, or judge others; rather, let them be meek, peaceful and unassuming, gentle and humble, speaking courteously to everyone, as is becoming. And they should not ride horseback unless they are forced by manifest necessity or infirmity. In whatever house they enter, let them say: Peace to this house. And, according to the holy Gospel, they are free to eat of whatever food is set before them.

Chapter IV: Against receiving money

I firmly command all the brothers that they in no way receive coins or money, either personally or through an intermediary. Nonetheless, let the ministers and custodians alone take special care to provide for the needs of the sick and the clothing of the other brothers through spiritual friends according to [diversity of] places and seasons and cold climates, as they may judge the demands of necessity; excepting always, as stated above, they do not receive coins or money.

Chapter V: The manner of working

Those brothers to whom the Lord has given the grace of working should do their work faithfully and devotedly so that, avoiding idleness (the enemy of the soul), they do not extinguish the spirit of holy prayer and devotion to which all other things of our earthly existence must contribute. As payment for their work they may receive whatever is necessary for their own bodily needs and [those of] their brothers, but not money in any form; and they should do this humbly as is fitting for servants of God and followers of most holy poverty.

Chapter VI: Against acquiring anything as one's own; begging alms; the sick brothers

The brothers shall not acquire anything as their own, neither a house nor a place nor anything at all. Instead, as pilgrims and strangers in this world who serve the Lord in poverty and humility, let them go begging for alms with full trust. Nor should they feel ashamed, since the Lord made Himself poor for us in this world. This is that summit of highest poverty which has established you, my most beloved brothers, as heirs and kings of the kingdom of heaven; it has made you poor in the things [of this world] but exalted you in virtue. Let this be your portion, which leads into the land of the living. Dedicating yourselves totally to this, my most beloved brothers, do not wish to have anything else forever under heaven for the sake of our Lord Jesus Christ.

And wherever the brothers may be together or meet [other] brothers, let them give witness that they are members of one family. And let each one confidently make known his need to the other, for if a mother has such care and love for her son born according to the flesh, should not someone love and care for his brother according to the Spirit even more diligently? And if any of them becomes sick, the other brothers should serve him as they would wish to be served themselves.

Chapter VII: The penance to be imposed on the brothers who sin

If any of the brothers, at the instigation of the enemy, sin mortally in regard to those sins about which it may have been decreed among the brothers to have recourse only to the ministers provincial, such brothers must have recourse to them as soon as possible, without delay. If these ministers are priests, they shall impose a penance upon them with mercy; but if they are not priests, they shall have it imposed by other priests of the order as it seems best to them according to God. They must take care not to become angry or disturbed because of the sin of another, since anger and disturbance hinder charity in themselves and in others.

Chapter VIII: The election of the minister general of this fraternity and the Chapter of Pentecost

All the brothers are bound always to have one of the brothers of this order as the minister general and servant of the entire fraternity, and they are bound strictly to obey him. Should he die, the election of a successor should be made by the ministers provincial and the custodians at the Chapter of Pentecost, for which the ministers provincial are always bound to convene in whatever place it has been decided by the minister general; and they shall do this once every three years or at a longer or shorter interval as decided by the aforesaid minister. And if at any time it should become evident to the body of the ministers provincial and the custodians that the aforesaid minister is not qualified for the service and general welfare of the brothers, then the same brothers, to whom the election is entrusted, are bound in the name of the Lord to elect another for themselves as custodian. After the Chapter of Pentecost each minister and custodian may call his brothers to a chapter once in the same year in their territories—if they wish and if it seems expedient to them.

Chapter IX: Preachers

The brothers shall not preach in the diocese of any bishop when he has opposed their doing so. And none of the brothers shall dare to preach to the people unless he has been examined and approved by the minister general of this fraternity and has received from him the office of preaching. I also admonish and exhort these brothers that, in their preaching, their words be well chosen and chaste, for the instruction and edification of the people, speaking to them of vices and virtues, punishment and glory in a discourse that is brief, because it was in few words that the Lord preached while on earth.

Chapter X: The admonition and correction of the brothers

The brothers who are the ministers and servants of the other brothers should visit and admonish their brothers and humbly and charitably correct them, not commanding them anything which might be against their conscience and our rule. On the other hand, the brothers who are subject to them should remember that they have given up their own wills for God. Therefore, I strictly command them to obey their ministers in all those things which they have promised the Lord to observe and which are not against [their] conscience and our rule. And wherever there are brothers who know and realize that they cannot observe the rule spiritually, it is their duty and right to go to the minister for help. The ministers on their part should receive them with great kindness and love and should be so approachable that these brothers can speak and deal with [the ministers] as masters with their servants; for this is the way it should be: the ministers shall be the servants of all the brothers. At the same time I admonish and exhort the brothers in the Lord Jesus Christ that they beware of all pride, vainglory, envy, avarice, cares and worries of this world, detraction, and complaint. And those who are illiterate should not be eager to learn. Instead, let them pursue what they must desire above all things: to have the Spirit of the Lord and His holy manner of working, to pray always to Him with a pure heart, to have humility, to have patience in persecution and weakness, and to love those who persecute us, find fault with us, or rebuke us, because the Lord says: Love your enemies, and pray for those who persecute and slander you [Matt. 5:44]. Blessed are those who suffer persecution for the sake of justice, for theirs is the kingdom of heaven [Matt. 5:10]. But whoever perseveres to the end, he will be saved [Matt. 10:22].

Chapter XI: Against entering the monasteries of nuns

I firmly command all the brothers not to have any associations or meetings with women which could arouse suspicion. Moreover, they should not enter the monasteries of nuns, except those [brothers] to whom special permission has been granted by the Apostolic See. They should not be godfathers of men or women so that scandal not arise on this account among the brothers or concerning them.

Chapter XII: Those who go among the Saracens and other nonbelievers

Those brothers who, by divine inspiration, desire to go among the Saracens and other nonbelievers should ask permission from their ministers provincial. But the ministers should not grant permission except to those whom they consider fit to be sent.

In addition, I command the ministers through obedience to petition the Lord Pope for one of the cardinals of the holy Roman Church, who would be the governor, protector, and corrector of this fraternity, so that, always submissive and prostrate at the feet of the same holy Church, and steadfast in the Catholic faith, we may observe the poverty and the humility and the holy Gospel of our Lord Jesus Christ which we have firmly promised.

No one, therefore, is in any way permitted to tamper with this decree of our confirmation or to oppose it rashly. If anyone should presume to attempt this, let it be known that he shall incur the indignation of Almighty God and of His blessed Apostles Peter and Paul.

Given at the Lateran, the twenty-ninth day of November, in the eighth year of our pontificate.

8. The Rule for Hermitages

The importance given to the eremitical (reclusive) spirit in the life of Saint Francis has not escaped students of his life throughout the centuries. His biographers are in agreement concerning his zeal in cultivating the solitary life and his pleasure with those friars who gave themselves to a life of seclusion to deepen their relationship with God.

The Rule for Hermitages expresses a spirit of simplicity and fraternity, reconciling the solitude of eremitical life with the brotherhood that is an essential characteristic of Franciscan life. When this document is examined against the background of the early biographies of Saint Francis, the eremitical manner of living described in it appears to be a symbol of the saint's inner life. Thus it is an invaluable tool in understanding the spirit of il Poverello.

Those who wish to live religiously in hermitages should be three brothers or four at the most; two of these should be "mothers," and they may have two sons or at least one. The two who are mothers should follow the life of Martha, while the two sons should follow the life of Mary, and they may have an enclosure in which each one may have his small cell in which he may pray and sleep. And they should always say Compline of the day immediately after sundown; and they should be eager to keep silence, and to say their hours, and to rise for Matins; and let them seek first of all the kingdom of God and His justice. And let them say Prime at the proper time, and after Terce they may be free from silence, and they may speak and go to their mothers. And, whenever it pleases them, they can seek alms from them as little poor ones, for the love of God. And afterward they should say Sext and None and Vespers at the proper time. And in the enclosure where they live, they should not permit any person to enter, nor should they eat there. Those brothers who are the mothers should be eager to stay far from every person; and because of the obedience to their minister they should protect their sons from everyone, so that no one can talk with them. And the sons should not talk with any person except with their mothers and with the minister and his custodian, when it pleases them to visit with the blessing of the Lord God. The sons, however, should sometimes assume the role of the mothers, as from time to time it may seem good to them to exchange [roles]. They should strive to observe conscientiously and carefully all the things mentioned above.

9. The Salutation of the Blessed Virgin Mary

In his Second Life of Saint Francis, Thomas of Celano describes the love of Saint Francis for the mother of Jesus as "inexpressible," for "it was she who made the Lord of majesty our brother." Saint Francis's simple litany describes Mary's role in the plan of salvation and uses many titles that were familiar to the medieval Christian to praise her unique position. Although the manuscript tradition suggests a close tie between this piece and the Salutation of the Virtues (which follows), it is more accurate to consider them as separate works. Nonetheless, Saint Francis clearly perceives and presents the Virgin Mary as the model for every Christian who responds to the virtuous presence of God in his life.

Hail, O Lady,
holy Queen,
Mary, holy Mother of God:
you are the Virgin made church
and the one chosen by the most holy Father in heaven
whom He consecrated
with His most holy beloved Son
and with the Holy Spirit the Paraclete,
in whom there was and is
all the fullness of grace and every good.
Hail, His Palace!
Hail, His Tabernacle!
Hail, His Home!
Hail, His Robe!

Hail, His Servant!
Hail, His Mother!
And, [hail] all you holy virtues
which through the grace and light of the Holy Spirit
are poured into the hearts of the faithful
so that from their faithless state
you may make them faithful to God.

10. The Salutation of the Virtues

The more one ponders this simple text, the more Saint Francis is revealed as a theologian of the workings of the Spirit and of divine grace in the soul of one who has surrendered himself entirely to God by "dying" to self to live totally for God.

Although the titles of this work differ in many early manuscripts, the authenticity of the text has been solidly established. Thomas of Celano witnessed to its existence when he quoted a section of it in his Second Life of Saint Francis.

The work can be divided into three major sections: the salutations addressed to the virtues, the dispositions necessary for their reception, and the description of each virtue's activity. The consideration of each of the virtues in a feminine sense is an expression of the medieval milieu from which this writing comes. What is curious, though, is the manner of linking certain virtues to one another. The combination established between wisdom and simplicity, poverty and humility, and love and obedience speaks eloquently of the unique vision of Saint Francis.

> Hail, Queen Wisdom, may the Lord protect you
> with your sister, holy pure Simplicity.
> Lady, holy Poverty, may the Lord protect you
> with your sister, holy Humility.
> Lady, holy Charity, may the Lord protect you
> with your sister, holy Obedience.
> O most holy Virtues, may the Lord protect all of you,
> from Whom you come and proceed.
> There is surely no one in the entire world
> who can possess any one of you unless he dies first.

Whoever possesses one [of you]

and does not offend the others

possesses all.

And whoever offends one [of you]

does not possess any

and offends all.

And each one destroys vices and sins.

Holy Wisdom destroys

Satan and all his subtlety.

Pure holy Simplicity destroys

all the wisdom of this world

and the wisdom of the body.

Holy Poverty destroys

the desire of riches and avarice

and the cares of this world.

Holy Humility destroys pride

and all the people who are in the world

and all things that belong to the world.

Holy Charity destroys

every temptation of the devil and of the flesh

and every carnal fear.

Holy Obedience destroys

every wish of the body and of the flesh

and binds its mortified body

to obedience of the Spirit

and to obedience of one's brother,

and [the person who possesses her] is subject and submissive to all persons in the world,

and not to man only

but even to all beasts and wild animals

so that they may do whatever they want with him

inasmuch as it has been given to them from

    above by the Lord.

11. The Testament of Saint Francis

Shortly before his death, in October 1226, Saint Francis dictated a document that he called "my testament" and declared that he was writing it "so that we may observe in a more Catholic manner the rule which we have promised to the Lord." Saint Francis expressly cautioned his followers against looking on this document as "another rule," since it was only a "remembrance" or an "admonition." Evidently he did not intend to endow the Testament with any legally binding force over and beyond the Rule of the Order of Friars Minor. Yet the work contains statements that go beyond mere exhortation and seem to lay down commands that are binding under obedience. Thus the Testament has become one of the most controversial documents to come to us from Saint Francis. At the same time, the Testament has always been held in great respect as an expression of the profound wisdom and vision of Saint Francis and of his care and concern for those who would follow him.

The Lord granted me, Brother Francis, to begin to do penance in this way: While I was in sin, it seemed very bitter to me to see lepers. And the Lord Himself led me among them and I had mercy upon them. And when I left them that which seemed bitter to me was changed into sweetness of soul and body; and afterward I lingered a little and left the world.

And the Lord gave me such faith in churches that I would simply pray and speak in this way: "We adore You, Lord Jesus Christ, in all Your churches throughout the world, and we bless You, for through Your holy cross You have redeemed the world."

Afterward the Lord gave me and still gives me such faith in priests who live according to the manner of the holy Roman

Church because of their order, that if they were to persecute me, I would [still] have recourse to them. And if I possessed as much wisdom as Solomon had and I came upon pitiful priests of this world, I would not preach contrary to their will in the parishes in which they live. And I desire to fear, love, and honor them and all others as my masters. And I do not wish to consider sin in them because I discern the Son of God in them and they are my masters. And I act in this way since I see nothing corporally of the most high Son of God in this world except His most holy body and blood which they receive and which they alone administer to others. And these most holy mysteries I wish to have honored above all things and to be reverenced and to have them reserved in precious places. Wherever I come upon His most holy written words in unbecoming places, I desire to gather them up and I ask that they be collected and placed in a suitable place. And we should honor and respect all theologians and those who minister the most holy divine words as those who minister spirit and life to us.

And after the Lord gave me brothers, no one showed me what I should do, but the Most High Himself revealed to me that I should live according to the form of the holy Gospel. And I had this written down simply and in a few words and the Lord Pope confirmed it for me. And those who came to receive life gave to the poor everything which they were capable of possessing and they were content with one tunic, patched inside and out, with a cord and short trousers. And we had no desire for anything more. We [who were] clerics used to say the office as other clerics did; the lay brothers said the Our Father; and we quite willingly stayed in churches. And we were simple and subject to all.

And I used to work with my hands, and I [still] desire to work; and I firmly wish that all my brothers give themselves to honest work. Let those who do not know how [to work] learn, not from desire of receiving wages for their work but as an example and in order to avoid idleness. And when we are not paid for our work, let us have recourse to the table of the Lord, seeking alms from door to door. The Lord revealed to me a greeting, as we used to say: "May the Lord give you peace."

Let the brothers beware that they by no means receive churches or poor dwellings or anything which is built for them, unless it is in harmony with [that] holy poverty which we have promised in the rule, [and] let them always be guests there as pilgrims and strangers. And I firmly command all of the brothers through obedience that, wherever they are, they should not be so bold as to seek any letter from the Roman Curia either personally or through an intermediary, neither for a church or for some other place or under the guise of preaching or even for the persecution of their bodies; but wherever they have not been received, let them flee into another country to do penance with the blessing of God.

And I firmly wish to obey the minister general of this fraternity and another guardian whom it might please him to give me. And I wish to be so captive in his hands that I cannot go [anywhere] or do [anything] beyond obedience and his will, for he is my master.

And although I may be simple and infirm, I wish nonetheless always to have a cleric who will celebrate the office for me as it is contained in the rule. And all the other brothers are bound to obey their guardians and to celebrate the office according to the rule. And [if] any are found who do not celebrate the office according to the rule and [who] wish to alter it in any way or [who] are not Catholics, let all the brothers be obliged through obedience that wherever they come upon [such a brother] they must bring him to the custodian [who is] nearest to that place where they have found him. And the custodian is strictly bound through obedience to guard him strongly as a prisoner day and night, so that he cannot be snatched from his hands until he can personally deliver him into the hands of his minister. And the minister is strictly bound through obedience to send him with brothers who shall guard him as a prisoner day and night until they deliver him before the Lord of Ostia, who is the master, protector, and corrector of the entire fraternity.

And let the brothers not say: This is another rule; because this is a remembrance, an admonition, an exhortation, and my testament, which I, little Brother Francis, prepare for all of you, my blessed brothers, so that we may observe in a more Catholic manner the rule which we have promised to the Lord.

And the minister general and all other ministers and custodians are bound through obedience not to add to or subtract from these words. And let them always have this writing with them along with the rule. And in all the chapters which they hold, when they read the rule, let them also read these words. And I through obedience strictly command all my brothers, cleric and lay, not to place glosses on the rule or on these words, saying: They are to be understood in this way. But as the Lord has granted me to speak and to write the rule and these words simply and purely, so shall you understand them simply and without gloss, and observe them with [their] holy manner of working until the end.

And whoever shall have observed these [things], may he be filled in heaven with the blessing of the most high Father and on earth with the blessing of His beloved Son with the most Holy Spirit the Paraclete and with all the powers of heaven and all the saints. And I, little brother Francis, your servant, inasmuch as I can, confirm for you this most holy blessing both within and without.

12. The Blessing Given to Brother Bernard

In his Life of Saint Francis, Saint Bonaventure described Bernard of Quin-
tavalle as the "firstborn son" of the saint. The lives of the two men were entwined
from the first days at the Portiuncula, through the trips to Rome and France
and Spain, to the moments of Francis's death. This blessing given to Brother
Bernard is taken from the description of the last moments of Saint Francis
found in The Legend of Perugia.

Write this just as I tell you: Brother Bernard was the first
brother whom the Lord gave me, as well as the first to put into
practice and fulfill most completely the perfection of the holy
Gospel by distributing all his goods to the poor; because of this
and many other prerogatives, I am bound to love him more than
any other brother of the entire order. Therefore, as much as I can,
I desire and command that, whoever the minister general is, he
should cherish and honor him as he would me, and likewise the
ministers provincial and the brothers of the entire order should
esteem him in place of me.

13. The Blessing Sent to Saint Clare and Her Sisters

The Legend of Perugia *narrates the sickness of Saint Clare during the last week of Saint Francis's life and her fear of dying without a final glimpse of the saint. Out of compassion for Clare and her sisters, Saint Francis dictated this blessing.*

To console her [Saint Francis] sent her in writing his blessing and likewise absolved her from any failure if she had committed any against his orders and wishes and the commands and wishes of the Son of God.

14. A Letter Written to Lady Jacoba

Lady Jacoba de'Settesoli became one of the prominent members of the Third Order (a group of secular Franciscans) and won the affectionate title "Brother Jacoba," by which Saint Francis made her famous in history. The Tract on the Miracles by Thomas of Celano and The Legend of Perugia tell us that Saint Francis had just finished dictating this final message to her when Lady Jacoba arrived with the very items the saint had requested.

The holy woman was discovered to have brought everything for the burial of her father which the letter written just a short time before had requested. For she brought an ashen-colored cloth with which the body of the deceased would be covered, many candles, a veil for [his] face, a little pillow for [his] head, and a certain sweetmeat which the saint had desired.

15. The Testament Written in Siena

Thomas of Celano's First Life of Saint Francis describes the physical condition of Saint Francis as deteriorating so rapidly that, while he was in Siena six months before his death, it looked as though death were imminent. The friars asked him for his blessing and an expression of his last will. The three simple points that Saint Francis left them reflect the three foundations of the heritage he gave his followers: fraternity, poverty, and obedience to the Church.

Write that I bless all my brothers, [those] who are in the order and [those] who will come until the end of the world.... Since because of my weakness and the pain of my sickness I am not strong enough to speak, I make known my will to my brothers briefly in these three phrases—namely, as a sign that they remember my blessing and my testament, let them always love one another, let them always love and be faithful to our Lady holy Poverty, and let them always be faithful and subject to the prelates and all clerics of holy Mother Church.

16. True and Perfect Joy

This is a different type of writing, since it is transmitted through the medium of a story and through a much later witness, a fourteenth-century manuscript. This description of perfect joy graphically portrays Saint Francis's understanding of true minority—humility, simplicity, and vulnerability—and expresses the Franciscan ideal through the medium of the human person.

[Brother Leonard] related, in the same place [the Portiuncula], that one day at Saint Mary the blessed Saint Francis called Brother Leo and said: "Brother Leo, write!" He answered: "I'm ready."

"Write," [Francis] said, "what true joy is." [And Brother Leo recorded his words:]

A messenger comes and says that all the masters in Paris have come into the order; write: This is not true joy. Or that all the prelates beyond the mountains [have entered the order], as well as the archbishops and bishops; or that the king of France and the king of England [have entered the order]; write: This is not true joy. Again, that my brothers have gone to the nonbelievers and converted all of them to the faith; again, that I have so much grace from God that I heal the sick and perform many miracles: I tell you that true joy does not consist in any of these things.

What then is true joy?

I return from Perugia and arrive here in the dead of night; and it is wintertime, muddy and so cold that icicles have formed on the edges of my habit and keep striking my legs, and blood flows from such wounds. And all covered with mud and cold, I come to the gate; and after I have knocked and called for some time, a brother comes and asks: "Who are you?" I answer: "Brother Francis." And he says: "Go away; this is not a proper hour for going about; you may not come in." And when I insist, he answers: "Go away, you are a simple and a stupid person; we are so many and we have no need of you. You are certainly not coming to us at this hour!" And I stand again at the door and say: "For the love of God, take me in tonight." And he answers: "I will not. Go to the Crosiers' place and ask there." I tell you this: If I had patience and did not become upset, there would be true joy in this and true virtue and the salvation of the soul.

PART TWO

�֍

The Writings of
Saint Clare

A BRIEF BIOGRAPHY OF SAINT CLARE OF ASSISI

Clare of Assisi was the founder of the Poor Clares, a community of women dedicated to poverty, simplicity, and service. Though she is less famous than Francis, her life illuminated the ideals of Franciscan life as beautifully and imaginatively as did his.

Clare was born to a noble family in Assisi in 1194 and was converted, under Francis's influence, in the year 1211. Accompanied by her aunt Bianca, she fled from her parents' home; she received the habit from Francis on March 18–19, 1212, in the Church of the Porziuncula. Her sister Agnes soon followed her into the religious life. So did her mother, Ortolana, and her sister Beatrice.

Many biographers tend to romanticize the friendship between Francis and Clare. Even discounting some embellishments regarding their relationship (in their own time and today), it remains true that Clare was one of Francis's most devoted followers.

The times she lived in were not as favorable to strongly apostolic roles for women as times had been several centuries earlier. Rather, the idea of an enclosed community of women was very much in the spirit of her generation, and Clare followed that path. In 1215 Clare was made superior of her community at San Damiano and remained the superior until her death.

Clare was ill and confined to a sickbed from 1224 onward; the exact nature of her illness is not known. This invalidism was a definite factor in shaping her ministry, as she was recognized for her holiness and her wide influence. Because of her devotion to the Holy Eucharist it was believed that her intercessory prayers had helped to spare Assisi from the attacks of the Saracens. Monasteries of Poor Clares sprang up around Europe even during her lifetime.

The Rule of her community met with many difficulties and was not approved until August 9, 1253, just two days before her death. After her death she was proclaimed a saint by the Roman Catholic Church.

The guiding value of the Poor Clares is a God-centered poverty, which is perceived not only as a lack of material goods but also as a spiritual dependence on God for everything. In granting "the privilege of poverty" to Clare and her community, Pope Gregory IX wrote as follows: "Finally, He who feeds the birds of the air and the lilies of the field will not fail you in both food and vesture until He Himself comes and serves you (Lk. 12:37) in eternity, when namely His right hand will embrace you in the fullness of His vision."

The Letters of Saint Clare to Blessed Agnes of Prague

Clare's four letters to *Agnes of Prague*, presented here, are invaluable expressions of the writer's spiritual wisdom as well as of her desire to guide another in the pursuit of evangelical perfection and profound poverty. These short pieces of literature are characterized by a beautiful, sensitive style and have become rich sources of the Franciscan spiritual heritage.

Agnes of Prague was born in 1203, the daughter of King Ottakar of Bohemia and Queen Constance of Hungary. In 1206, when she was only three years old, Agnes was betrothed to Boleslaus, son of Henry, duke of Silesia, and Hedwig of Bavaria, who was later canonized. A short time afterward, Boleslaus died and the young girl was sought after by Emperor Frederick II, who desired to have her as a bride for his son and, some years later, for himself. Neither union was to be.

In 1232 Agnes came to know the Friars Minor, who had visited Prague on a preaching tour. Within a short time she built a church, a friary, and a hospital dedicated to Saint Francis and became enamored of the spiritual life the friars revealed to her. On June 11, 1234—Pentecost Sunday—Agnes entered the monastery that was attached to the hospital and began to correspond with Clare, whose life and spirit she desired to emulate. Agnes remained in this monastery for almost half a century, during which time she struggled to maintain many of the same expressions of the religious life that Clare did. She died on March 2, 1282, and was beatified by Pope Pius IX in 1874.

1. The First Letter to Blessed Agnes of Prague

This letter from Clare was written before Agnes's entrance into religious life. The embrace of such a difficult way of life must have attracted a great deal of attention, as a letter written by Pope Gregory IX to Agnes, dated August 30, 1234, indicates. Clare, in the letter below, uses the phrase "known not only to me but to the entire world as well" in describing Agnes's "holy conduct and irreproachable life." An echo of this phrase is found in a papal bull sent to Beatrice of Castile, June 5, 1235, in which the same pope presents an enthusiastic praise of the princess of Bohemia. Thus Clare's letter offers respect and reverence, as well as an encouraging set of contrasts between the life of earthly royalty and the life of the kingdom of heaven.

> To the esteemed and most holy virgin, the Lady Agnes, daughter of the most excellent and illustrious king of Bohemia: Clare, an unworthy servant of Jesus Christ and useless handmaid of the Cloistered Ladies of the Monastery of San Damiano, her subject and servant in all things, presents herself totally with a special reverent [prayer] that she attain the glory of everlasting happiness.

As I hear of the fame of your holy conduct and irreproachable life, which is known not only to me but to the entire world as well, I greatly rejoice and exult in the Lord. I am not alone in rejoicing at such great news, but [I am joined by] all who serve and seek to serve Jesus Christ. For, though you, more than others, could have enjoyed the magnificence and honor and dignity of the world, and could have been married to the illustrious Caesar with splendor befitting you and His Excellency, you have rejected all these things and have chosen with your whole heart and soul a life of holy poverty and destitution. Thus you took a spouse of a more noble lineage, Who will keep your virginity ever unspotted and unsullied, the Lord Jesus Christ:

> When you have loved [Him], you shall be chaste;
> when you have touched [Him], you shall become pure;
> when you have accepted [Him], you shall be a virgin.
> Whose power is stronger,
> Whose generosity is more abundant,
> Whose appearance more beautiful,
> Whose love more tender,
> Whose courtesy more gracious.
> In Whose embrace you are already caught up;
> Who has adorned your breast with precious stones
> and has placed priceless pearls in your ears
> and has surrounded you with sparkling gems
> as though blossoms of springtime
> and placed on your head a golden crown
> as a sign [to all] of your holiness.

Therefore, most beloved sister, or should I say, lady worthy of great respect: because you are the spouse and the mother and the sister of my Lord Jesus Christ, and have been adorned resplendently with the sign of inviolable virginity and most holy poverty, be strengthened in the holy service which you have undertaken out of an ardent desire for the Poor Crucified, Who for the sake of all of us took upon Himself the Passion of the cross and delivered us from the power of the Prince of Darkness to whom we were enslaved because of the disobedience of our first parent, and so reconciled us to God the Father.

> O blessed poverty,
> who bestows eternal riches on those who love and
>   embrace her!
> O holy poverty,
> to those who possess and desire you
> God promises the kingdom of heaven
> and offers, indeed, eternal glory and blessed life!
> O God-centered poverty,
> whom the Lord Jesus Christ
> Who ruled and now rules heaven and earth,
> Who spoke and things were made,
> condescended to embrace before all else!

The foxes have dens, He says, and the birds of the air have nests, but the Son of Man, Christ, has nowhere to lay His head, but bowing His head gave up His spirit.

If so great and good a Lord, then, on coming into the Virgin's womb, chose to appear despised, needy, and poor in this world, so that people who were in utter poverty and want and in absolute need of heavenly nourishment might become rich in Him by possessing the kingdom of heaven, then rejoice and be glad! Be filled with a remarkable happiness and a spiritual joy! Contempt of the world has pleased you more than [its] honors, poverty more than earthly riches, and you have sought to store up greater treasures in heaven rather than on earth, where rust does not consume nor moth destroy nor thieves break in and steal. Your reward, then, is very great in heaven! And you have truly merited to be called a sister, spouse, and mother of the Son of the Father of the Most High and of the glorious Virgin.

You know, I am sure, that the kingdom of heaven is promised and given by the Lord only to the poor: for he who loves temporal things loses the fruit of love. Such a person cannot serve God and Mammon, for either the one is loved and the other hated, or the one is served and the other despised.

You also know that one who is clothed cannot fight with another who is naked, because he is more quickly thrown who gives his adversary a chance to get hold of him; and that one who lives in the glory of earth cannot rule with Christ in heaven.

Again, [you know] that it is easier for a camel to pass through the eye of a needle than for a rich man to enter the kingdom of heaven. Therefore, you have cast aside your garments—that is, earthly riches—so that you might not be overcome by the one fighting against you, [and] that you might enter the kingdom of heaven through the straight path and the narrow gate.

What a great laudable exchange:

> to leave the things of time for those of eternity,
> to choose the things of heaven for the goods of earth,
> to receive the hundredfold in place of one,
> and to possess a blessed and eternal life.

Because of this I have resolved, as best I can, to beg Your Excellency and Your Holiness by my humble prayers in the mercy of Christ, to be strengthened in His holy service, and to progress from good to better, from virtue to virtue, so that He Whom you serve with the total desire of your soul may bestow on you the reward for which you long.

I also beg you in the Lord, as much as I can, to include in your holy prayers me, your servant, though unworthy, and the other sisters with me in the monastery, who are all devoted to you, so that by their help we may merit the mercy of Jesus Christ, and together with you may merit to enjoy the everlasting vision.

Farewell in the Lord. And pray for me.

2. The Second Letter to Blessed Agnes of Prague

An early edition of this letter, which was discovered in a convent in Prague, contains the heading "Concerning the Strong Perseverance in a Good Proposal." The text of the letter suggests its composition during the early years of Agnes's religious life, when Brother Elias was minister general of the friars. It delicately provides Agnes of Prague with the principal means of perseverance in her commitment to poverty: a life of loving contemplation on Christ.

To the daughter of the King of kings, the servant of the Lord of lords, the most worthy spouse of Jesus Christ, and, therefore, the most noble queen, Lady Agnes: Clare, the useless and unworthy servant of the Poor Ladies: greetings and [a wish for your] perseverance in a life of the highest poverty.

I give thanks to the Giver of grace from Whom, we believe, every good and perfect gift proceeds, because He has adorned you with such splendors of virtue and signed you with such marks of perfection that, since you have become such a diligent imitator of the Father of all perfection, His eyes do not see any imperfection in you.

This is the perfection which will prompt the King Himself to take you to Himself in the heavenly bridal chamber where He is seated in glory on a starry throne because you have despised the splendors of an earthly kingdom and considered of little value the offers of an imperial marriage. Instead, as someone zealous for the holiest poverty, in the spirit of great humility and the most ardent charity, you have held fast to the footprints of Him to Whom you have merited to be joined as a spouse.

But since I know that you are adorned with many virtues, I will spare my words and not weary you with needless speech, even though nothing seems superfluous to you if you can draw from it some consolation. But because one thing alone is necessary, I bear witness to that one thing and encourage you, for love of Him to Whom you have offered yourself as a holy and pleasing sacrifice, that, like another Rachel, you always remember your resolution and be conscious of how you began.

What you hold, may you [always] hold.
What you do, may you [always] do and never abandon.
But with swift pace, light step,
[and] unswerving feet,
so that even your steps stir up no dust,
go forward
securely, joyfully, and swiftly,
on the path of prudent happiness,
believing nothing,
agreeing with nothing
which would dissuade you from this resolution
or which would place a stumbling block for you on the way,
so that you may offer your vows to the Most High
in the pursuit of that perfection
to which the Spirit of the Lord has called you.

In all of this, follow the counsel of our venerable father, our Brother Elias, the minister general, so that you may walk more securely in the way of the commands of the Lord. Prize it beyond the advice of the others and cherish it as dearer to you than any gift. If anyone would tell you something else or suggest something which would hinder your perfection or seem contrary to your divine vocation, even though you must respect him, do not follow his counsel. But as a poor virgin, embrace the poor Christ.

Look upon Him Who became contemptible for you, and follow Him, making yourself contemptible in the world for Him. Your spouse, though more beautiful than the children of men, became, for your salvation, the lowest of men, despised, struck, scourged untold times throughout His whole body, and then died amid the sufferings of the cross. O most noble queen, gaze upon [Him], consider [Him], contemplate [Him], as you desire to imitate [Him].

If you suffer with Him, you shall reign with Him;
[if you] weep [with Him], you shall rejoice with Him;
[if you] die [with Him] on the cross of tribulation,
you shall possess heavenly mansions in the splendor of the saints
and, in the Book of Life, your name shall be called glorious among men.

Because of this you shall share always and forever the glory of the kingdom of heaven in place of earthly and passing things, and everlasting treasures instead of those that perish, and you shall live forever.

Farewell, most dear sister, yes, and lady, because of the Lord, your spouse. Commend me and my sisters to the Lord in your fervent prayers, for we rejoice in the good things of the Lord that He works in you through His grace.

Commend us truly to your sisters as well.

3. The Third Letter to Blessed Agnes of Prague

The immediate cause of this letter was a clarification requested of Clare by Agnes concerning fasting and abstinence. In a papal bull of February 9, 1237, Pope Gregory IX had mandated "total abstinence from meat in imitation of the Cistercians." Furthermore, in January 1238 Agnes had petitioned the pope for a rule similar to that followed by the Poor Ladies of San Damiano in Assisi. This request was denied on May 11, 1238. Thus this response of Clare may have been an encouragement to Agnes to persevere in her life of prayer, poverty, and austerity, which play an important role in the Church.

> To the lady [who is] most respected in Christ and the sister loved more than all [other] human beings, Agnes, sister of the illustrious king of Bohemia, but now the sister and spouse of the most high King of heaven: Clare, the most lowly and unworthy handmaid of Christ and servant of the Poor Ladies: the joys of redemption in the Author of salvation and every good thing that can be desired.

I am filled with such joys at your well-being, happiness, and marvelous progress through which, I understand, you have advanced in the course you have undertaken to win the prize of heaven. And I sigh with such happiness in the Lord because I know you see that you make up most wonderfully what is lacking both in me and in the other sisters in following the footprints of the poor and humble Jesus Christ.

I can rejoice truly—and no one can rob me of such joy—
because I now possess what under heaven I have desired. For I see
that, helped by a special gift of wisdom from the mouth of God
Himself and in an awe-inspiring and unexpected way, you have
brought to ruin the subtleties of our crafty enemy and the pride that
destroys human nature and the vanity that infatuates human hearts.

I see, too, that by humility, the virtue of faith, and the strong
arms of poverty, you have taken hold of that incomparable treasure
hidden in the field of the world and in the hearts of men, with
which you have purchased that field of Him by Whom all things
have been made from nothing. And, to use the words of the
Apostle himself in their proper sense, I consider you a co-worker
of God Himself and a support of the weak members of His ineffable Body. Who is there, then, who would not encourage me to
rejoice over such marvelous joys?

Therefore, dearly beloved, may you too always rejoice in the
Lord. And may neither bitterness nor a cloud [of sadness] over-
whelm you, O dearly beloved lady in Christ, joy of the angels and
crown of your sisters!

> Place your mind before the mirror of eternity!
> Place your soul in the brilliance of glory!
> Place your heart in the figure of the divine substance!
> And transform your whole being into the image of the
>   Godhead Itself through contemplation!
> So that you too may feel what His friends feel
> as they taste the hidden sweetness

which God Himself has reserved from the beginning
for those who love Him.

Since you have cast aside all [those] things which, in this
deceitful and turbulent world, ensnare their blind lovers, love
Him totally Who gave Himself totally for your love. His beauty
the sun and moon admire; and of His gifts there is no limit in
abundance, preciousness, and magnitude. I am speaking of Him
Who is the Son of the Most High, Whom the Virgin brought to
birth and remained a virgin after His birth. Cling to His most
sweet Mother who carried a Son Whom the heavens could not
contain; and yet she carried Him in the little enclosure of her
holy womb and held Him on her virginal lap.

Who would not dread the treacheries of the enemy of
mankind, who, through the arrogance of momentary and deceptive glories, attempts to reduce to nothing that which is greater
than heaven itself? Indeed, is it not clear that the soul of the faithful person, the most worthy of all creatures because of the grace
of God, is greater than heaven itself? For the heavens with the rest
of creation cannot contain their Creator. Only the faithful soul is
His dwelling place and [His] throne, and this [is possible] only
through the charity which the wicked do not have. [He Who is]
the Truth has said: Whoever loves Me will be loved by My Father,
and I too shall love him, and We shall come to Him and make our
dwelling place with Him.

Therefore, as the glorious Virgin of virgins carried [Christ]
materially in her body, you too, by following in His footprints—

especially [those] of poverty and humility—can, without any doubt, always carry Him spiritually in your chaste and virginal body. And you will hold Him by Whom you and all things are held together, [thus] possessing that which, in comparison with the other transitory possessions of this world, you will possess more securely. How many kings and queens of this world let themselves be deceived! For, even though their pride may reach the skies and their heads through the clouds, in the end they are as forgotten as a dung-heap!

Now concerning those matters which you have asked me to clarify for you: which are the specific feasts our most glorious Father Saint Francis urged us to celebrate in a special way by a change of food, feasts of which, I believe, you already have some knowledge—I propose to respond to your love.

Your prudence should know then that, except for the weak and the sick, for whom [Saint Francis] advised and admonished us to show every possible care in matters of food, none of us who are healthy and strong should eat anything other than Lenten fare, either on ferial days or on feast days. Thus, we must fast every day except Sundays and the Nativity of the Lord, on which days we may have two meals. And on ordinary Thursdays everyone may do as she wishes, so that she who does not wish to fast is not obliged. However, we who are well should fast every day except on Sundays and on Christmas.

During the entire Easter week, as the writing of Saint Francis tells us, and on the feast days of the blessed Mary and of the holy Apostles, we are not obliged to fast, unless these feasts occur on a

Friday. And, as I have already said, we who are well and strong always eat Lenten fare.

But our flesh is not bronze nor is our strength that of stone. No, we are frail and inclined to every bodily weakness! I beg you, therefore, dearly beloved, to refrain wisely and prudently from an indiscreet and impossible austerity in the fasting that I know you have undertaken. And I beg you in the Lord to praise the Lord by your very life, to offer to the Lord your reasonable service, and your sacrifice always seasoned with salt.

May you do well in the Lord, as I hope I myself do. And remember me and my sisters in your prayers.

4. The Fourth Letter to Blessed Agnes of Prague

It is difficult to determine the date of the composition of this letter. Certainly a long time has elapsed since the sending of the previous letter, for Clare herself suggests an infrequent exchange of letters due to a scarcity of messengers and the dangers of travel. An indication of the date, however, is given at the conclusion as Clare writes that her blood sister, Agnes, who had been in a convent in Monte-celli, had returned to San Damiano. (Agnes had returned to be with her sister in 1253, the year of Clare's death.) Thus this letter was written during the last months of Clare's life and reflects the brilliant spirit of love that permeated all of her religious life.

> To her who is the half of her soul and the special shrine of
> her heart's deepest love, to the illustrious queen and bride
> of the Lamb, the eternal King: to the Lady Agnes, her most
> dear mother, and, of all the others, her favorite daughter:
> Clare, an unworthy servant of Christ and a useless hand-
> maid of His handmaids in the Monastery of San Damiano
> of Assisi: health and [a prayer] that she may sing a new
> song with the other most holy virgins before the throne
> of God and of the Lamb and follow the Lamb wherever
> He may go.

O mother and daughter, spouse of the King of all ages, if I have not written to you as often as your soul and mine as well desire and long for, do not wonder or think that the fire of love for you glows less sweetly in the heart of your mother. No, this is the difficulty: the lack of messengers and the obvious dangers of the roads. Now, however, as I write to your love, I rejoice and exult with you in the joy of the Spirit, O bride of Christ, because, since you have totally abandoned the vanities of this world, like another most holy virgin, Saint Agnes, you have been marvelously espoused to the spotless Lamb Who takes away the sins of the world.

> Happy, indeed, is she to whom it is given to share this
>   sacred banquet,
> to cling with all her heart to Him
> Whose beauty all the heavenly hosts admire unceasingly,
> Whose love inflames our love,
> Whose contemplation is our refreshment,
> Whose graciousness is our joy,
> Whose gentleness fills us to overflowing,
> Whose remembrance brings a gentle light,
> Whose fragrance will revive the dead,
> Whose glorious vision will be the happiness
> of all the citizens of the heavenly Jerusalem.

Inasmuch as this vision is the splendor of eternal glory, the brilliance of eternal light, and the mirror without blemish, look upon that mirror each day, O queen and spouse of Jesus Christ, and continually study your face within it, so that you may adorn yourself within and without with beautiful robes and cover yourself with the flowers and garments of all the virtues, as becomes the daughter and most chaste bride of the most high King. Indeed, blessed poverty, holy humility, and ineffable charity are reflected in that mirror, as, with the grace of God, you can contemplate them throughout the entire mirror.

Look at the parameters of this mirror—that is, the poverty of Him Who was placed in a manger and wrapped in swaddling clothes. O marvelous humility, O astonishing poverty! The King of the angels, the Lord of heaven and earth, is laid in a manger! Then, at the surface of the mirror, dwell on the holy humility, the blessed poverty, the untold labors and burdens which He endured for the redemption of all mankind. Then, in the depths of this same mirror, contemplate the ineffable charity which led Him to suffer on the wood of the cross and die thereon the most shameful kind of death. Therefore, that Mirror, suspended on the wood of the cross, urged those who passed by to consider, saying: All you who pass by the way, look and see if there is any suffering like My suffering! [Lam 1:12]. Let us answer Him with one voice and spirit, as He said: Remembering this over and over leaves my soul downcast within me! [Lam. 3:20]. From this moment, then, O queen of our heavenly King, let yourself be inflamed more strongly with the fervor of charity!

[As you] contemplate further His ineffable delights, eternal riches and honors, and sigh for them in the great desire and love of your heart, may you cry out:

Draw me after You!
We will run in the fragrance of Your perfumes,
O heavenly Spouse!

> I will run and not tire,
> until You bring me into the wine cellar,
> until Your left hand is under my head
> and Your right hand will embrace me happily
> [and] You will kiss me with the happiest kiss of Your mouth.

In this contemplation, may you remember your poor little mother, knowing that I have inscribed the happy memory of you indelibly on the tablets of my heart, holding you dearer than all the others.

What more can I say? Let the tongue of the flesh be silent when I seek to express my love for you; and let the tongue of the Spirit speak, because the love that I have for you, O blessed daughter, can never be fully expressed by the tongue of the flesh, and even what I have written is an inadequate expression.

I beg you to receive my words with kindness and devotion, seeing in them at least the motherly affection which in the fire of charity I feel daily toward you and your daughters, to whom I warmly commend myself and my daughters in Christ. On their part, these very daughters of mine, especially the most prudent virgin Agnes, our sister, recommend themselves in the Lord to you and your daughters.

Farewell, may dearest daughter, to you and to your daughters until we meet at the throne of the glory of the great God, and desire [this] for us.

Inasmuch as I can, I recommend to your charity the bearers of this letter, our dearly beloved Brother Amatus, beloved of God and men, and Brother Bonagura. Amen.

5. The Letter to Ermentrude of Bruges

Luke Wadding wrote in 1257 that Clare penned two letters to Ermentrude of Bruges, who had founded several monasteries in Flanders that sought to live after the manner of the Poor Ladies of San Damiano in Assisi. However, Wadding presented only one text, which appears to be a summary of both letters. The chronicler did not indicate what manuscript or text he had at hand. This letter is much more simple and impersonal than the other writings of Clare, which has caused scholars to doubt its authenticity.

> To her dearest Sister Ermentrude: Clare of Assisi, a lowly servant of Jesus Christ: health and peace.

I have learned, O most dear sister, that with the help of God's grace you have fled in joy the corruptions of the world. I rejoice and congratulate you because of this and, again, I rejoice that you are walking courageously the paths of virtue with your daughters. Remain faithful until death, dearly beloved, to Him to Whom you have promised yourself, for you shall be crowned by Him with the garland of life.

Our labor here is brief, but the reward is eternal. Do not be disturbed by the clamor of the world, which passes like a shadow. Do not let the false delights of a deceptive world deceive you. Close your ears to the whisperings of hell and bravely oppose its onslaughts. Gladly endure whatever goes against you and do not let good fortune lift you up: for these things destroy faith, while these others demand it. Offer faithfully what you have vowed to God, and He shall reward you.

O dearest one, look up to heaven, which calls us on, and take up the cross and follow Christ Who has gone on before us: for through Him we shall enter into His glory after many and diverse tribulations. Love God from the depths of your heart and Jesus, His Son, Who was crucified for us sinners. Never let the thought of Him leave your mind but meditate constantly on the mysteries of the cross and the anguish of His Mother as she stood beneath the cross.

Pray and watch at all times! Carry out steadfastly the work you have begun and fulfill the ministry you have undertaken in true humility and holy poverty. Fear not, daughter! God, Who is faithful in all His words and holy in all His deeds, will pour His blessings upon you and your daughters. He will be your help and best comforter, for He is our Redeemer and our eternal reward.

Let us pray to God together for each other, for by sharing each other's burden of charity in this way, we shall easily fulfill the law of Christ.

Amen.

6. The Rule of Saint Clare

At the beginning of her religious life, Clare received a pattern of life from Father Francis, whom she considered her mentor and guide. It is not evident that that pattern contained any detailed prescriptions for the life professed by Clare and her sisters; the only knowledge we have of its content is the small fragment that Clare herself presented in the sixth chapter of her rule. We do know, however, that three years after her conversion she declined the name and office of abbess and chose to be a subject. Nonetheless, at the urging of Saint Francis, Clare took on the responsibility of that role, but she considered it a service rather than an honor.

During Clare's time, it was customary for new religious communities to follow the established rule of an existing community. For three decades the Poor Ladies of San Damiano followed a version of the Rule of Saint Benedict assigned to them by the cardinal archbishop of Ostia and Velletri. Then, in 1247, Pope Innocent IV wrote a second, modified rule for the Poor Ladies. Neither rule, however, contained the practice of intense poverty that Clare considered the heart of her religious commitment.

Clare began to write her own rule, which was officially approved by Cardinal Rainaldo di Segni, the protector of the Poor Ladies, on September 16, 1252. One year later, on August 9, 1253, two days before her death, Clare received word of the papal bull that gave final approval to her rule. The original document was delivered to her on her deathbed, and according to an annotation added to the parchment at a later date, she kissed it many times.

> Innocent, bishop, servant of the servants of God, to the
> beloved daughters in Christ the Abbess Clare and the other

sisters of the Monastery of San Damiano in Assisi: our best wishes and apostolic blessing.

The Apostolic See is accustomed to accede to the pious requests and to be favorably disposed to grant the praiseworthy desires of its petitioners. Thus, we have before us your humble request that we confirm by [our] apostolic authority the form of life which blessed Francis gave you and which you have freely accepted. According to [this form of life], you are to live together in unity of mind and heart and in the profession of highest poverty. Our venerable brother, the bishop of Ostia and Velletri, has seen fit to approve this way of life, as the bishop's own letters on this matter define more fully; and we have taken care to strengthen it with our apostolic protection. Attentive, therefore, to your devout prayers, we approve and ratify what the bishop has done in this matter and confirm it by apostolic authority and support it by this document. To this end we include herein the text of the bishop, which is the following:

Raynaldus, by divine mercy bishop of Ostia and Velletri, to his most dear mother and daughter in Christ, the Lady Clare, abbess of San Damiano in Assisi, and to her sisters, both present and to come, greetings and fatherly blessings.

Beloved daughters in Christ, because you have rejected the splendors and pleasures of the world and, following the foot-prints of Christ Himself and His most holy Mother, you have chosen to live in the cloister and to serve the Lord in highest poverty so that, in freedom of soul, you may be the Lord's servants, we approve your holy way of life in the Lord and with fatherly affection we desire freely to impart our benign favor to your wishes and holy desires. Therefore, moved by your pious prayers and by the authority of the Lord Pope as well as our own, to all of you who are now in your monastery and to all those who will succeed you we confirm forever this form of life and the manner of holy unity and highest poverty which your blessed Father Saint Francis gave you for your observance in word and writing. Furthermore, by the protection of this writing, we fortify this way of life which is the following:

Chapter I: Beginning the form of life of the Poor Sisters in the name of the Lord

The form of life of the Order of the Poor Sisters [i.e., the Poor Ladies] which the blessed Francis established is this: to observe the holy Gospel of our Lord Jesus Christ, by living in obedience, without anything of one's own, and in chastity.

Clare, the unworthy handmaid of Christ and the little plant of the most blessed Father Francis, promises obedience and reverence to the Lord Pope Innocent and to his canonically elected successors, and to the Roman Church. And, just as at the beginning of her conversion, together with her sisters, she promised obedience to the blessed Francis, so now she promises his successors to observe the same [obedience] inviolably. And the other sisters shall always be obliged to obey the successors of the

blessed Francis and [to obey] Sister Clare and the other canonically elected abbesses who shall succeed her.

Chapter II: Those who wish to accept this life and how they are to be received

If, by divine inspiration, anyone should come to us with the
desire to embrace this life, the abbess is required to seek the consent of all the sisters; and if the majority shall have agreed, having had the permission of our cardinal protector, she can receive
her. And if she judges [the candidate] acceptable, let [the abbess]
carefully examine her, or have her examined, concerning the
Catholic faith and the sacraments of the Church. And if she
believes all these things and is willing to profess them faithfully
and to observe them steadfastly to the end; and if she has no
husband, or if she has [a husband] who has already entered religious life with the authority of the bishop of the diocese and has
already made a vow of continence; and if there is no impediment to the observance of this life, such as advanced age or some
mental or physical weakness, let the tenor of our life be clearly
explained to her.

And if she is suitable, let the words of the holy Gospel be
addressed to her: that she should go and sell all that she has and
take care to distribute the proceeds to the poor. If she cannot do
this, her good will suffices. And let the abbess and her sisters take
care not to be concerned about her temporal affairs, so that she
may freely dispose of her possessions as the Lord may inspire her.
If, however, some counsel is required, let them send her to some

prudent and God-fearing men, according to whose advice her goods may be distributed to the poor.

Afterward, once her hair has been cut off round her head and her secular dress set aside, she is to be allowed three tunics and a mantle. Thereafter, she may not go outside the monastery except for some useful, reasonable, evident, and approved purpose. When the year of probation is ended, let her be received into obedience, promising to observe always our life and form of poverty.

During the period of probation no one is to receive the veil. The sisters may also have small cloaks for convenience and propriety in serving and working. Indeed, the abbess should provide them with clothing prudently, according to the needs of each person and place, and seasons and cold climates, as it shall seem expedient to her by necessity.

Young girls who are received into the monastery before the age established by law should have their hair cut round [their heads]; and, laying aside their secular dress, should be clothed in religious garb as the abbess has seen [fit]. When, however, they reach the age required by law, in the same way as the others, they may make their profession. The abbess shall carefully provide a mistress from among the more prudent sisters of the monastery, both for these and for the other novices. She shall form them diligently in a holy manner of living and proper behavior according to the form of our profession.

In the examination and reception of the sisters who serve outside the monastery, the same form as above is to be observed. These sisters may wear shoes. No one is to live with us in the monastery unless she has been received according to the form of our profession.

And for the love of the most holy and beloved Child Who was wrapped in the poorest of swaddling clothes and laid in a manger, and of His most holy Mother, I admonish, entreat, and exhort my sisters that they always wear the poorest of garments.

Chapter III: The Divine Office; fasting, confession, and Communion

The sisters who can read shall celebrate the Divine Office according to the custom of the Friars Minor; for this they may have breviaries, but they are to read it without singing. And those who, for some reasonable cause, sometimes are not able to read and pray the hours may, like the other sisters, say the Our Fathers.

Those who do not know how to read shall say twenty-four Our Fathers for Matins; five for Lauds; for each of the hours of Prime, Terce, Sext, and None, seven; for Vespers, however, twelve; for Compline, seven. For the dead, let them also say seven Our Fathers with the *Requiem aeternam* in Vespers; for Matins, twelve: because the sisters who can read are obliged to recite the Office of the Dead. However, when a sister of our monastery shall have departed this life, they are to say fifty Our Fathers.

The sisters are to fast at all times. On Christmas, however, no matter on what day it falls, they may eat twice. The younger sisters, those who are weak, and those who are serving outside the monastery may be dispensed mercifully as the abbess sees fit. But in a time of evident necessity the sisters are not bound to corporal fasting.

At least twelve times a year they shall go to confession, with the permission of the abbess. And they shall take care not to introduce other talk unless it pertains to confession and the salvation of souls. They should receive Communion seven times [a year]— namely, on Christmas, Thursday of Holy Week, Easter, Pentecost, the Assumption of the Blessed Virgin, the Feast of Saint Francis, and the Feast of All Saints. [In order] to give Communion to the sisters who are in good health or to those who are ill, the chaplain may celebrate inside [the enclosure].

Chapter IV: The election and office of the abbess; the chapter; those who hold office and the discreets

In the election of the abbess the sisters are bound to observe the canonical form. However, they should arrange with haste to have present the minister general or the minister provincial of the Order of Friars Minor. Through the word of God he will dispose them to perfect harmony and to the common good in the choice they are to make. And no one is to be elected who is not professed. And if a nonprofessed should be elected or otherwise given them, she is not to be obeyed unless she first professes our form of poverty.

At the time of her death the election of another abbess is to take place. Likewise, if at any time it should appear to the entire body of the sisters that she is not competent for their service and common welfare, the sisters are then bound to elect another as abbess and mother as soon as possible, according to the form given above.

The one who is elected should reflect upon the kind of burden she has undertaken, and to Whom she is to render an account of the flock committed to her. She should strive as well to preside over the others more by her virtues and holy behavior than by her office, so that, moved by her example, the sisters might obey her more out of love than out of fear. She should avoid particular friendships, lest by loving some more than others she cause scandal among all. She should console those who are afflicted, and be, likewise, the last refuge for those who are disturbed; for, if they fail to find in her the means of health, the sickness of despair might overcome the weak.

She should preserve the common life in everything, especially regarding all in the church, dormitory, refectory, and infirmary, and in clothing. Her vicar is bound to do likewise.

At least once a week the abbess is required to call her sisters together in chapter. There both she and her sisters must confess their common and public offenses and negligences humbly. There, too, she should consult with all her sisters on whatever concerns the welfare and good of the monastery; for the Lord often reveals what is best to the lesser [among us].

No heavy debt is to be incurred except with the common consent of the sisters and by reason of an evident need. This should be done through a procurator. The abbess and her sisters, however, should be careful that nothing is deposited in the monastery for safekeeping; often such practices give rise to troubles and scandals.

To preserve the unity of mutual love and peace, all who hold offices in the monastery should be chosen by the common consent of all the sisters. And in the same way at least eight sisters are to be elected from among the more prudent, whose counsel the abbess is always bound to heed in those things which our form of life requires. Moreover, if it seems useful and expedient, the sisters can and must sometimes depose the officials and discreets and elect others in their place.

Chapter V: Silence in the church, in the parlor, and at the grille

The sisters are to keep silence from the hour of Compline until Terce, except those who are serving outside the monastery. They should also keep silence continually in the church, in the dormitory, and, only while they are eating, in the refectory. In the infirmary, however, they may speak discreetly at all times for the recreation and service of those who are sick. However, they may briefly and quietly communicate what is really necessary always and everywhere.

The sisters may not speak in the parlor or at the grille without the permission of the abbess or her vicar. And those who have permission should not dare to speak in the parlor unless they are in the presence and hearing of two sisters. Moreover, they should not presume to go to the grille unless there are at least three sisters present [who have been] appointed by the abbess or her vicar from the eight discreets who were elected by all the sisters as the council of the abbess. The abbess and her vicar are themselves bound to observe this custom in speaking. [The sisters should speak] very rarely at the grille, and by all means never at the door.

At the grille a curtain is to be hung inside which is not to be removed except when the word of God is being preached, or when a sister is speaking to someone. The grille should also have a wooden door which is well provided with two distinct iron locks, bolts, and bars, so that, especially at night, it can be locked by two keys, one of which the abbess is to keep and the other the sacristan; it is to be locked always except when the Divine Office is being celebrated and for reasons given above. Under no circumstances whatever is any sister to speak to anyone at the grille before sunrise or after sunset. Moreover, in the parlor there is always to be a curtain on the inside, which is never to be removed.

During the Lent of Saint Martin and the Greater Lent, no one is to speak in the parlor, except to the priest for confession or for some other evident necessity; judgment on this is left to the prudence of the abbess or her vicar.

Chapter VI: Not having possessions

After the most high celestial Father saw fit to enlighten my heart by His grace to do penance according to the example and teaching of our most blessed Father Saint Francis, shortly after his own conversion, I, together with my sisters, voluntarily promised him obedience.

When the blessed Father [Francis] saw that we had no fear of poverty, hard work, suffering, shame, or the contempt of the world, but that, instead, we regarded such things as great delights, moved by compassion he wrote for us a form of life as follows:

"Since by divine inspiration you have made yourselves daughters and servants of the most high King, the heavenly Father, and have taken the Holy Spirit as your spouse, choosing to live according to the perfection of the holy Gospel, I resolve and promise for myself and for my brothers always to have that same loving care and special solicitude for you as [I have] for them."

And that we might never turn aside from the most holy poverty we had embraced, [nor those, either, who would come after us], shortly before his death he wrote his last will for us once more, saying: "I, Brother Francis, the little one, wish to follow the life and poverty of our most high Lord Jesus Christ and of His most holy Mother and to persevere in this until the end; and I ask and counsel you, my ladies, to live always in this most holy life and in poverty. And keep most careful watch that you never depart from this by reason of the teaching or advice of anyone."

And just as I, together with my sisters, have been ever solicitous to safeguard the holy poverty which we have promised the Lord God and the blessed Francis, so, too, the abbesses who shall succeed me in office and all the sisters are bound to observe it inviolably to the end—that is to say, they are not to receive or hold onto any possessions or property [acquired] through an intermediary, or even anything that might reasonably be called property, except as much land as necessity requires for the integrity and the proper seclusion of the monastery; and this land is not to be cultivated except as a garden for the needs of the sisters.

Chapter VII: The manner of working

The sisters to whom the Lord has given the grace of working are to work faithfully and devotedly, [beginning] after the hour of Terce, at work which pertains to a virtuous life and to the common good. They must do this in such a way that, while they banish idleness, the enemy of the soul, they do not extinguish the spirit of holy prayer and devotion to which all other things of our earthly existence must contribute.

And the abbess or her vicar is bound to assign at the chapter, in the presence of all, the manual work each is to perform. The same is to be done if alms have been sent by anyone for the needs of the sisters, so that the donors may be remembered by all in prayer together. And all such things are to be distributed for the common good by the abbess or her vicar with the advice of the discreets.

Chapter VIII: Not acquiring anything as one's own; begging alms; the sick sisters

The sisters shall not acquire anything as their own, neither a house nor a place nor anything at all; instead, as pilgrims and strangers in this world who serve the Lord in poverty and humility, let them send confidently for alms. Nor should they feel ashamed, since the Lord made Himself poor for us in this world. This is that summit of highest poverty which has established you, my dearest sisters, as heirs and queens of the kingdom of heaven; it has made you poor in the things [of this world] but has exalted you in virtue. Let this be your portion, which leads into the land of the living. Dedicating yourselves totally to this, my most beloved sisters, do not wish to have anything else forever under heaven for the name of our Lord Jesus Christ and His most holy Mother.

No sister is permitted to send letters or to receive anything or give away anything outside the monastery without the permission of the abbess. Nor is it allowed to have anything which the abbess has not given or permitted. Should anything be sent to a sister by her relatives or others, the abbess should have it given to the sister. If she needs it, the sister may use it; otherwise, let her in all charity give it to a sister who does need it. If, however, money is sent to her, the abbess, with the advice of the discreets, may provide for the sister what she needs.

Regarding the sisters who are ill, the abbess is strictly bound to inquire with all solicitude by herself and through other sisters what [these sick sisters] may need by way both of counsel and of food and other necessities; and according to the resources of the place, she is to provide for them charitably and kindly. [This is to be done] because all are obliged to serve and provide for their sisters who are ill just as they would wish to be served themselves if they were suffering from any infirmity. Each should make known her needs to the other with confidence. For if a mother loves and nourishes her daughter according to the flesh, how much more lovingly must a sister love and nourish her sister according to the Spirit!

Those who are ill may lie on sackcloth filled with straw and may use feather pillows for their head; and those who need woolen stockings and quilts may use them.

When the sick sisters are visited by those who enter the monastery, they may answer them briefly, each responding with some good words to those who speak to them. But the other sisters who have permission [to speak] may not dare to speak to those who enter the monastery unless [they are] in the presence and hearing of two sister-discreets assigned by the abbess or her vicar. The abbess and her vicar, too, are obliged themselves to observe this manner of speaking.

Chapter IX: The penance to be imposed on the sisters who sin; the sisters who serve outside the monastery

If any sister, at the instigation of the enemy, shall have sinned mortally against the form of our profession, and if, after having been admonished two or three times by the abbess or other sisters, she will not amend, she shall eat bread and water on the floor before all the sisters in the refectory for as many days as she has been obstinate; and if it seems advisable to the abbess she shall undergo even greater punishment. Meanwhile, as long as she remains obstinate, let her pray that the Lord will enlighten her heart to do penance. The abbess and her sisters, however, must beware not to become angry or disturbed on account of anyone's sin: for anger and disturbance prevent charity in oneself and in others.

If it should happen—God forbid—that through [some] word or gesture an occasion of trouble or scandal should ever arise between sister and sister, let her who was the cause of the trouble at once, before offering the gift of her prayer to the Lord, not only prostrate herself humbly at the feet of the other and ask pardon, but also beg her earnestly to intercede for her to the Lord that He might forgive her. The other sister, mindful of that word of the Lord, If you do not forgive from the heart, neither will your heavenly Father forgive you [Matt. 6:15; 18:35], should generously pardon her sister every wrong she has done her.

The sisters who serve outside the monastery should not delay long outside unless some evident necessity demands it. They should conduct themselves virtuously and speak little, so that those who see them may always be edified. And let them zealously avoid all meetings or dealings that could be called into question. They may not be godmothers of men or women lest gossip or trouble arise because of this. They may not dare to repeat the rumors of the world inside the monastery. And they are strictly bound not to repeat outside the monastery anything that was said or done within which could cause scandal.

If anyone should on occasion openly offend in these two things, it shall be left to the prudence of the abbess to impose a penance on her with mercy. But if a sister does this through vicious habit, the abbess, with the advice of the discreets, should impose a penance on her according to the seriousness of her guilt.

Chapter X: The admonition and correction of the sisters

The abbess should admonish and visit her sisters, and humbly and charitably correct them, not commanding them anything which would be against their soul and the form of our profession. The sisters, however, who are subjects, should remember that for God's sake they have renounced their own wills. Hence, they are firmly bound to obey their abbess in all things which they promised the Lord to observe and which are not against their soul and our profession.

On her part, the abbess is to be so familiar with them that they can speak and act toward her as ladies do with their servant. For that is the way it should be, that the abbess be the servant of all the sisters.

Indeed, I admonish and exhort in the Lord Jesus Christ that the sisters be on their guard against all pride, vainglory, envy, greed, worldly care and anxiety, detraction and murmuring, dissension and division. Let them be ever zealous to preserve among themselves the unity of mutual love, which is the bond of perfection.

And those who do not know how to read should not be eager to learn. Rather, let them devote themselves to what they must desire to have above all else: the Spirit of the Lord and His holy manner of working—to pray always to Him with a pure heart, to have humility, [to have] patience in difficulty and weakness, and to love those who persecute, blame, and accuse us; for the Lord says: Blessed are they who suffer persecution for justice's sake, for theirs is the kingdom of heaven [Matt.5:10]. But he who shall have persevered to the end will be saved [Matt.10:22].

Chapter XI: The custody of the enclosure

The portress is to be mature in her manners, prudent, and of suitable age. During the day she should remain in an open cell without a door. A suitable companion should be assigned to her who may, whenever necessary, take her place in all things.

The door is to be well secured by two different iron locks, with bars and bolts, so that, especially at night, it may be locked with two keys, one of which the portress is to have, the other the abbess. And during the day the door must not be left unguarded on any account, but should be firmly locked with one key.

They should take utmost care to make sure that the door is never left open, except when this can hardly be avoided gracefully. And by no means shall it be opened to anyone who wishes to enter, except to those who have been granted permission by the Supreme Pontiff or by our Lord Cardinal. The sisters shall not allow anyone to enter the monastery before sunrise or to remain within after sunset, unless an evident, reasonable, and unavoidable cause demands otherwise.

If a bishop has permission to offer Mass within the enclosure, either for the blessing of an abbess or for the consecration of one of the sisters as a nun or for any other reason, he should be satisfied with as few and virtuous companions and assistants as possible.

Whenever it is necessary for other men to enter the monastery to do some work, the abbess shall carefully post a suitable person at the door who is to open it only to those assigned for the work, and to no one else. At such times all the sisters should be extremely careful not to be seen by those who enter.

Chapter XII: The visitator, the chaplain, and the cardinal protector

Our visitator, according to the will and command of our cardinal, should always be taken from the Order of Friars Minor. He should be the kind of person who is well known for his virtue and good life. It shall be his duty to correct any excesses against the form of our profession, whether these be in the leadership or among the members. Taking his stand in a public place, so that he can be seen by others, he may speak with several in a group and with individuals about the things that pertain to the duty of visitation, as it may seem best to him.

With respect for the love of God and of blessed Francis, we ask as a favor from the Order of Friars Minor a chaplain and a clerical companion of good character and reputation and prudent discretion, and two lay brothers who are lovers of holiness of life and virtue, to support us in our [life of] poverty, just as we have always had [them] through the kindness of the order.

The chaplain may not be permitted to enter the monastery without his companion. And when they enter, they are to remain in an open place, in such a way that they can see each other always and be seen by others. For the confession of the sick who cannot go to the parlor, for their Communion, for the last anointing and the prayers for the dying, they are allowed to enter the enclosure.

Moreover, for funeral services and on the solemnity of Masses for the dead, for digging or opening a grave, or also for making arrangements for it, suitable and sufficient outsiders may enter according to the prudence of the abbess.

To see to all these things above, the sisters are firmly obliged to have always that cardinal of the holy Church of Rome as our governor, protector, and corrector who has been delegated by the Lord Pope for the Friars Minor, so that, always submissive and

subject at the feet of that holy Church, and steadfast in the
Catholic faith, we may observe forever the poverty and humility
of our Lord Jesus Christ and of His most holy Mother and the
holy Gospel which we have firmly promised. Amen.

Given at Perugia, on the sixteenth day of September, in the tenth year of the
pontificate of the Lord Pope Innocent IV.

Therefore, no one is permitted to destroy this page of our confirmation or to
oppose it recklessly. If anyone shall have presumed to attempt this, let him know
that he will incur the wrath of Almighty God and of His holy Apostles Peter
and Paul.

Given at Assisi, on the ninth day of August, in the eleventh year of our
pontificate.

7. The Testament of Saint Clare

This text forms a beautiful autobiographical reflection of Saint Clare. No other writing of the saint—with the exception of the sixth chapter of her rule—speaks so eloquently about the origins of the Poor Ladies of San Damiano, the bond of unity between the Poor Ladies and Saint Francis and his brothers, and the love of poverty and humility that is the life of the "Little Flock" raised up by Father Francis to follow the footprints of Christ in the Church. Yet the Testament of Saint Clare is certainly one of the most controversial texts, in that its authenticity has been frequently brought into doubt. Nonetheless, it is a magnificent source of the spirituality of Saint Clare from which many valuable insights can be gained.

In the name of the Lord!

Among all the other gifts which we have received and continue to receive daily from our Benefactor, the Father of mercies, and for which we must express the deepest thanks to our glorious God, our vocation is a great gift. Since it is the more perfect and greater, we should be so much more thankful to Him for it. For this reason the Apostle writes: Acknowledge your calling [1 Cor. 1:26]. The Son of God became for us the Way which our blessed Father Francis, His true lover and imitator, has shown and taught us by word and example.

Therefore, beloved sisters, we must consider the immense gifts which God has bestowed on us, especially those which He has seen fit to work in us through His beloved servant, our blessed Father Francis, not only after our conversion but also while we were still [living among] the vanities of the world.

For almost immediately after his conversion, while he had neither brothers nor companions, when he was building the Church
of San Damiano in which he was totally filled with divine consolation, he was led to abandon the world completely. This holy
man, in the great joy and enlightenment of the Holy Spirit, made
a prophecy about us which the Lord fulfilled later. Climbing the
wall of that church, he shouted in French to some poor people
who were standing nearby: "Come and help me build the
Monastery of San Damiano, because ladies will dwell here who
will glorify our heavenly Father throughout His holy Church by
their celebrated and holy manner of life."

In this, then, we can consider the abundant kindness of God
toward us. Because of His mercy and love, He saw fit to speak
these words about our vocation and selection through His saint.
And our most blessed Father [Francis] prophesied not only for
us, but also for those who were to come to this [same] holy vocation to which the Lord has called us.

With what solicitude and fervor of mind and body, therefore,
must we keep the commandments of our God and Father, so that,
with the help of the Lord, we may return to Him an increase of
His talents. For the Lord Himself has set us as an example and
mirror not only for others, but also for our [own] sisters whom
the Lord has called to our way of life, so that they in turn will be
a mirror and example to those living in the world. Since, therefore, the Lord has called us to such great things, that those who
are to be models and mirrors for others may behold themselves
in us, we are truly bound to bless and praise the Lord and to be

strengthened constantly in Him to do good. Therefore, if we have lived according to the form [of life] given us, we shall, by very little effort, leave others a noble example and gain the prize of eternal happiness.

After the most high heavenly Father saw fit in His mercy and grace to enlighten my heart to do penance according to the example and teaching of our most blessed Father Francis, shortly after his own conversion, I, together with the few sisters whom the Lord had given me soon after my conversion, voluntarily promised him obedience, since the Lord had given us the light of His grace through his holy life and teaching.

But when the blessed Francis saw that, although we were physically weak and frail, we did not shirk deprivation, poverty, hard work, distress, or the shame or contempt of the world—rather, as he and his brothers often saw for themselves, we considered [all such trials] as great delights after the example of the saints and their brothers—he rejoiced greatly in the Lord. And moved by compassion for us, he promised to have always, both through himself and through his Order [of Friars Minor], the same loving care and special solicitude for us as for his own brothers.

And thus, by the will of God and our most blessed Father Francis, we went to dwell at the Church of San Damiano. There, in a short time, the Lord increased our number by His mercy and grace so that what He had predicted through His saint might be fulfilled. We had stayed in another place [before this], but only for a little while.

Later on he wrote a form of life for us, [indicating] especially that we should persevere always in holy poverty. And while he was living, he was not content to encourage us by many words and examples to love and observe holy poverty; [in addition] he also gave us many writings so that, after his death, we should in no way turn away from it. [In a similar way] the Son of God never wished to abandon this holy poverty while He lived in the world, and our most blessed Father Francis, following His footprints, never departed, either in example or in teaching, from this holy poverty which he had chosen for himself and for his brothers.

Therefore, I, Clare, the handmaid of Christ and of the Poor Sisters of the Monastery of San Damiano—although unworthy— and the little plant of the holy Father [Francis], consider together with my sisters our most high profession and the command of so great a father. [We also take note] in some [sisters] of the frailty which we feared in ourselves after the death of our holy Father Francis, [he] who was our pillar of strength and, after God, our one consolation and support. [Thus] time and again we bound ourselves to our Lady, most holy Poverty, so that, after my death, the sisters present and to come would never abandon her.

And, as I have always been most zealous and solicitous to observe and to have the other sisters observe the holy poverty which we have promised the Lord and our holy Father Francis, so, too, the others who will succeed me in office should be bound always to observe it and have it observed by the other sisters. And, for even greater security, I took care to have our profession of most holy poverty, which we promised our Father [Francis], strengthened with privileges by the Lord Pope Innocent, during whose pontificate we had our beginning, and by his other successors. [We did this] so that we would never nor in any way depart from it.

For this reason, on bended knees and with all possible respect, I commend all my sisters, both those present and those to come, to our holy mother the Church of Rome, to the supreme pontiff, and especially to the Lord Cardinal who has been appointed [protector] for the Order of Friars Minor and for us. [Inspired by] the love of the Lord Who was poor as He lay in the crib, poor as He lived in the world, Who remained naked on the cross, may [our protector] always see to it that his little flock observe that which [our] Lord [and] Father has begotten in His holy Church by the word and example of our blessed Father Francis, who followed the poverty and humility of His beloved Son and His glorious Virgin Mother—namely, holy poverty, which we have promised God and our most blessed Father Francis. May [our Lord Cardinal] always encourage and support [the sisters] in these things.

The Lord gave us our most blessed Father Francis as founder, planter, and helper in the service of Christ and in the things we have promised to God and to himself as our father. While he was living he was always solicitous in word and in deed to cherish and take care of us, his little plant. For these reasons I commend my sisters, both those present and those to come, to the successor of our blessed Father Francis and to the entire order, so that they may always help us to progress in serving God more perfectly and above all to observe most holy poverty in a more perfect manner.

If these sisters should ever leave this place and go elsewhere, after my death, wherever they may be, they are bound nonetheless to observe that form of poverty which we have promised God and our most blessed Father Francis. Nonetheless, let both the sister who is in office and the other sisters exercise such care and far-sightedness that they do not acquire or receive more land around the place than strict necessity requires for a vegetable garden. But if, for the integrity and privacy of the monastery, it becomes necessary to have more land beyond the limits of the garden, no more should be acquired than strict necessity demands. This land should not be cultivated or planted but always remain untouched and undeveloped.

In the Lord Jesus Christ, I admonish and exhort all my sisters, both those present and those to come, to strive always to imitate the way of holy simplicity, humility, and poverty and [to preserve] the integrity of [our] holy manner of life, as we were taught by our blessed Father Francis from the beginning of our conversion to Christ. Thus may they always remain in the fragrance of a good name, both among those who are afar off and those who are near. [This will take place] not by our own merits but solely by the mercy and grace of our Benefactor, the Father of mercies.

Loving one another with the charity of Christ, let the love you have in your hearts be shown outwardly in your deeds so that, compelled by such an example, the sisters may always grow in love of God and in charity for one another.

I also beg that sister who will have the office [of caring for] the sisters to strive to exceed others more by her virtues and holy life than by her office so that, encouraged by her example, the sisters may obey her not so much out of duty but rather out of love.

Let her also be prudent and attentive to her sisters just as a good mother is to her daughters; and especially, let her take care to provide for them according to the needs of each one from the things which the Lord shall give. Let her also be so kind and so available that all [of them] may reveal their needs with trust and have recourse to her at any hour with confidence as they see fit, both for her sake and that of her sisters.

But the sisters who are subjects should keep in mind that for the Lord's sake they have given up their own wills. Therefore, I ask that they obey their mother as they have promised the Lord of their own free will so that, seeing the charity, humility, and unity they have toward one another, their mother might bear all the burdens of her office more lightly. Thus what is painful and bitter might be turned into sweetness for her because of their holy way of life.

And because the way and path is straight and the gate through which one passes and enters into life is narrow, there are few who walk on it and enter through it. And if there are some who walk that way for a time, there are very few who persevere in it. How blessed are those to whom it has been given to walk that way and persevere to the end!

Therefore, as we have set out on the path of the Lord, let us take care that we do not turn away from it by our own fault or negligence or ignorance, nor that we offend so great a Lord and His Virgin Mother, and our [earthly] father, the blessed Francis, and the Church triumphant and, indeed, the Church militant. For it is written: Cursed are those who turn away from Your commandments [Ps. 118:21].

For this reason I bend my knees to the Father of our Lord Jesus Christ, that through the prayers and merits of the glorious and holy Virgin Mary, His Mother, and of our most blessed Father Francis and all the saints, the Lord Himself Who has given us a good beginning will [also] give the increase and constant perseverance to the end. Amen.

So that it may be observed better, I leave this writing for you, my dearest and most beloved sisters, those present and those to come, as a sign of the blessing of the Lord and of our most blessed Father Francis and of my blessing—I who am your mother and servant.

8. The Blessing Attributed to Saint Clare

The thirteenth-century Legend of Saint Clare portrays the last hour of the saint's earthly life. As she was dying, Clare blessed her sisters at San Damiano, as well as those in other monasteries and those who would come in the future. It is impossible to determine whether this narration gave rise to the tradition of a special blessing attributed to Saint Clare. There is also some evidence of a special blessing that Saint Clare sent to Agnes of Prague. It is similar to that blessing of the dying saint. The earliest known text of this blessing, found in a Middle High German translation, dates to about 1350. No study of the work has been able to determine its authenticity. Yet the tradition of the Poor Clares has always cherished this text as a precious remembrance of their foundress.

> In the name of the Father and of the Son and of the Holy Spirit. Amen.
>
> May the Lord bless you and keep you. May He show His face to you and be merciful to you. May He turn His countenance to you and give you peace.
>
> I, Clare, a handmaid of Christ, a little plant of our holy Father Francis, a sister and mother of you and the other Poor Sisters, although unworthy, ask our Lord Jesus Christ through His mercy and through the intercession of His most holy Mother Mary, of blessed Michael the Archangel and all the holy angels of God, and of all His men and women saints, that the heavenly Father give you and confirm

for you this most holy blessing in heaven and on earth. On earth, may He increase [His] grace and virtues among His servants and handmaids of His Church militant. In heaven, may He exalt and glorify you in His Church triumphant among all His men and women saints.

I bless you in my life and after my death as much as I can and more than I can with all the blessings with which the Father of mercies has and will have blessed His sons and daughters in heaven and on earth. Amen.

Always be lovers of God and your souls and the souls of your sisters, and always be eager to observe what you have promised the Lord.

May the Lord be with you always; and wherever you are, may you be with Him always. Amen.

ABOUT THE EDITOR

HarperCollins Spiritual Classics Series Editor Emilie Griffin has long been interested in the classics of the devotional life. She has written a number of books on spiritual formation and transformation, including *Clinging: The Experience of Prayer* and *Wilderness Time: A Guide to Spiritual Retreat*. With Richard J. Foster she coedited *Spiritual Classics: Selected Readings on the Twelve Spiritual Disciplines*. Her latest book is *Wonderful and Dark Is this Road: Discovering the Mystic Path*. She is a board member of Renovaré and leads retreats and workshops throughout the United States. She and her husband William live in Alexandria, Louisiana.

ABOUT MICHAEL MORRIS

Michael Morris is the author of the acclaimed novels *A Place Called Wiregrass*, winner of the 2003 Christy Award for Best First Novel, and *Slow Way Home*. Morris is also the author of a novella based on the Grammy nominated song *Live Like You Were Dying*. He lives with his wife, Melanie, in Alabama.

THE CLASSICS OF **WESTERN SPIRITUALITY**
A LIBRARY OF THE GREAT SPIRITUAL MASTERS

These volumes contain original writings of universally acknowledged teachers within the Catholic, Protestant, Eastern Orthodox, Jewish, Islamic, and American Indian traditions.

The Classics of Western Spirituality unquestionably provide the most in-depth, comprehensive, and accessible panorama of Western mysticism ever attempted. From the outset, the Classics has insisted on the highest standards for these volumes, including new translations from the original languages, and helpful introductions and other aids by internationally recognized scholars and religious thinkers, designed to help the modern reader to come to a better appreciation of these works that have nourished the three monotheistic faiths for centuries.

For more information on the
CLASSICS OF WESTERN SPIRITUALITY, contact Paulist Press
(800) 218-1903 • **www.paulistpress.com**